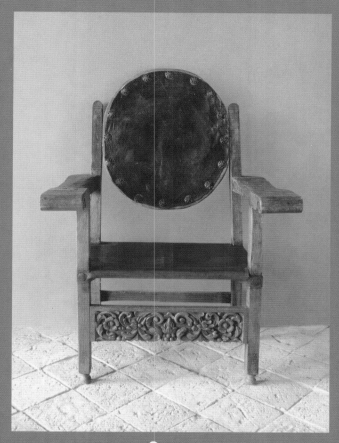

HACIENDA
STYLE

HACIENDA STYLE

KAREN WITYNSKI
JOE P. CARR

PHOTOGRAPHY BY KAREN WITYNSKI

Gibbs Smith, Publisher
TO ENRICH AND INSPIRE HUMANKIND
Salt Lake City | Charleston | Santa Fe | Santa Barbara

For my mother, Judith Simpson; sisters Amy Witynski Holmes, Mara Witynski and Jenny Witynski and brothers-in-law, Marion Holmes, Jeff Schramm for their tremendous love and support.

First Edition

11 10 09 08 07   5 4 3 2 1

Text © 2007 by Karen Witynski and Joe P. Carr

Photographs © 2007 by Karen Witynski

Published by

Gibbs Smith, Publisher

P.O. Box 667

Layton, Utah 84041

Orders: 1.800.835.4993

www.gibbs-smith.com

Designed by CN Design

Printed and bound in China

Library of Congress Cataloging-in-Publication Data

Witynski, Karen [date]-

  Hacienda style / Karen Witynski and Joe P. Carr; photographs by Karen Witynski. — 1st ed.

     p. cm.

  ISBN-13: 978-1-4236-0000-8

    1. Haciendas—Mexico. 2. Interior decoration—Mexico. 3. Architecture—Mexico I. Carr, Joe P., [date]- II. Title.

  NA8206.M6W58 2007

  728'.370972—dc22

  2006021955

Contents

FRONT COVER: At Merimo Nah, pomegranate-hued walls are a dramatic backdrop for a colonial painting. Restoration and design by Salvador Reyes Ríos and Josefina Larraín.

HALF TITLE: An antique Mexican armchair features an ornately-carved wood panel. Collection of the authors, Joe P. Carr and Karen Witynski.

PAGE 2: A Mexican cypress ranch table and antique ceramic grace this colorful záguan. Hacienda Granada. Home of the authors, Joe P. Carr and Karen Witynski.

TITLE PAGE: An antique Mexican door panel features simple, elegant carving.

CONTENTS PAGE: An old Mexican armoire dating from the late eighteenth century features handpainted designs. Collection of the authors, Joe P. Carr and Karen Witynski.

THIS PAGE: Inspired by the lockplates on old colonial trunks, this iron wall sconce features masterful ironwork. Home of the authors, Joe P. Carr and Karen Witynski, Hacienda Granada.

PAGE 8: An ornate stencil graces the walls of a restored Yucatán hacienda.

BACK COVER: The inviting steps at Hacienda Chimay are carpeted with the blooms of majestic flamboyan trees.

Acknowledgments

Many dear people contributed generously to this book, sharing their creativity, support and enthusiasm.

We are grateful to our friends in Mexico, the homeowners, architects, designers, artists and craftsmen who have shared their knowledge and spirited hospitality over the years. Their tremendous talent and innovation were the inspiration for this volume.

A heartfelt thanks to the people who were an integral part of shaping this book. First, to my sister Amy Witynski Holmes for her help in editing the manuscript. Her masterful writing talent and enthusiasm made the word journey an enjoyable adventure. We thank our art director, Christine Nasser, for her great design talent, and most of all, her special friendship; our agent and friend Betsy Amster, for her expert advice and special support; and the Gibbs Smith team, including editors Madge Baird and Carrie Westover, for their valuable insight and continued dedication to our Mexican book series.

We acknowledge with gratitude the assistance of the Government of the State of Yucatán, the Governor, Mr. Patricio Patrón Laviada; the Secretary of Tourism, Carolina Cárdenas Sosa; Public Relations Director, Ana Argáez Escalante, who shared her expert knowledge; Carlos Baqueiro; and Luis Ernesto Villanueva Chac, whose assistance and creativity was invaluable to our photo shoots.

We are particularly grateful to our dear friends and colleagues, Salvador Reyes Ríos and Josefina Larraín who generously shared their knowledge and whose design talents so enriched this book. Additional thanks to Salvador for writing the foreword and his enthusiastic assistance with the manuscript.

We wish to express our thanks to the many friends and associates who contributed their valuable efforts to this book: Jen Lytle, who continues to inspire us with her passion for Mexico and great knowledge of colonial homes; Travis Smith for his expert technical assistance; Alvaro Ponce; Roberto Cardenas and Eduardo Cardenas; Manolo Vega; Tomas Pacheco and Ignacio Durán Encalada for their great insight and kindness.

Additional thanks to the following pioneers who lent valuable support: Roberto Hernández, Claudia Madrazo, Marilu Hernández, Luis Bosoms, Patricia Wohler, Luis Millet and Carlos Millet.

We would also like to thank the following people who hospitably opened their homes and haciendas to us: Dr. Hernán and Mayo Patrón, Mr. and Mrs. Leanardo Silveria Cuevas, Luis and Laura de Yturbe, Jim Neeley and David Dow, Howie and Cyndy Burger, Raymond Branham, Isabelle Kimmelman, Ed Holler and Sam Saunders, David Sterling and Keith Heitke, Daniel and Sofi Bosco, Philipe and Dominique Duneton, Fritz Menzel and Werner Gross, Arturo Sanchez, Silviane Boucher, Fiona St. Clair, George Fischer and Sam Woodruff, Joanne Andrews, Christopher Holder and Wiggie Andrews, Ron and Silvia Jackson, Deborah LaChapelle, Bob and Carole Gow, Claude and Monique Forget, Amelia Lara Tamburrino, Octavio Monsalve Uribe, Manolo and Aurora Vega, Jaime Barrera Aguilar, Ana Beatriz Parizot Wolter, Jim and Nancy Swickard.

Our gratitude to those who gave insightful advice and help, among them Dr. Luis Castaneda, Nely Argulo, Dr. José Yacaman, Alejandro Chan Casanova. A most sincere thank you to Roberto Girotti and Olga Rubio for their special support of the book.

Many thanks to our friends at La Misión de Fray Diego: Luis Florencia, Ruben Aguilar Massoni, Mayanin Herrera, Sonia Pasos, Manuel Valladares, Humberto Gutierrez, Eduardo Barrera.

A special note of appreciation to those special individuals who assisted us while on location, including: Rene Nieto, Tatiana Cervera, Francisco Loría Mafud, Beatriz Nino and Belen Llin, Roman Canche P., Juan Kantun Puc, Abelardo Noh Tun, Raul Narvaez and Alberto Narvaez, Pedro Nipsch. Special thanks to Luis Villanueva Chac and his wonderful family: Omar and Irene, Omar and Anita, Carlos, Roberto, Manuel, Selma and Joel for their special kindness and support.

Finally, our deep appreciation to our families for their constant support, my mother Judith M. Simpson, sisters Amy Witynski Holmes, Mara Witynski and Jenny Witynski, and brothers-in-law, Marion Holmes and Jeff Schramm. A special tribute to Joe P. Carr Sr., Joe Carr III, Michael Carr, Jim and Mary Ellen Emery, and Verne and Beverly Dwyer for their continued support.

We would like to acknowledge Continental Airlines for their support with air transportation during our research trips to Mexico.

Special thanks to La Misíon de Fray Diego for providing us with wonderful accommodations and great service while in Mérida.

Foreword

For several decades and from several places in Mexico, the architecture and infrastructure of the old haciendas have become a vast fountain of inspiration and applied knowledge for architects, artists and designers. During the seventeenth to nineteenth and early twentieth centuries, the multifaceted activities in the various types of haciendas resulted in an expansive range of practical and aesthetic architectural solutions that reflect both time and the spirit of the particular site. What these buildings express is an authentic identity united with environmental, climatic, and landscape conditions—an identity born of lessons the older generation extracted from centuries of interaction with nature. This confluence marks the hacienda's architectural evolution as cultural and historical places that unlock an important part of the Mexican soul.

For owners or designers, consideration of the authentic identity of a historical property is an important issue necessary before restoration or renovation, especially when the renovation introduces new uses and architectural spaces. Thus proceeding, in the midst of projecting a new spirit and personality upon it, we will be led to the path of authentic preservation of the original character of the old building.

This part of the Mexican soul needs to be understood in order to be re-created. It is more critical in the case of new residential construction which seeks to recall the "hacienda style" and be original at the same time. Luis Barragán and a few architects and designers have succeeded in recent years in achieving this understanding of a building's soul.

Old buildings are frequently open books that clamor for a detailed reading. At the least, a survey and minimal historical research are the required tools to embark on a serious approach to renovation. These prerequisites will provide a heightened sensibility to the site's architectural elements and composition, as well as to the original constructive materials and construction systems. In terms of architecture and interior design, a fusion between the old and the new styles is only feasible from these bases.

As an architect-designer focused in restoration-renovation work, I have led significant projects that fused restoration with new building uses. Among my projects in the last ten years are the resurrection of several sisal haciendas, as well as old, turn-of-the-century houses in Mérida, the capital of Yucatán.

Along with this book's authors, my design partner and wife, Josefina Larraín, as well as many other contributing individuals, we define ourselves as promoters of the creativity and diffusion of Mexican soul, and of the pulse of the Mexican architectural-style renaissance. In *Hacienda Style*, the images and text reveal an important angle of the homes and haciendas that comprise part of this renaissance.

Following *Casa Yucatán*, which came to life in 2002, Karen Witynski and Joe P. Carr have again taken on the challenge of condensing a valuable, updated panorama of what particular owners and designers are doing to evolve Mexican hacienda style to the present time. *Hacienda Style* is their new invitation to join all of them.

—Salvador Reyes Ríos

Introduction

WITH A VAST ARCHITECTURAL LEGACY SPANNING FOUR CENTURIES, MEXICAN HACIENDAS EXPRESS A RUGGED, ROMANTIC BEAUTY AND A COMPELLING SENSE OF HISTORY. FIRST APPEARING IN NEW SPAIN SHORTLY AFTER THE CONQUEST IN 1521, THE HACIENDA SYSTEM ORIGINATED AS LAND GRANTS AWARDED BY THE KING OF SPAIN TO LOCAL CONQUISTADORS AND SPANISH ELITE IN EXCHANGE FOR MILITARY AND SOCIAL SERVICES TO THE CROWN. DERIVED FROM THE SPANISH VERB HACER, MEANING "TO DO," THE HACIENDA HAS BEEN THE ECONOMIC BACKBONE OF RURAL MEXICO THROUGHOUT ITS HISTORY. THE TYPE OF PRODUCTION AND ARCHITECTURAL STYLE VARIED ACCORDING TO THE HACIENDA'S MOMENT IN TIME, GEOGRAPHICAL REGION AND NATURAL RESOURCES. PREDOMINATELY DEDICATED TO AGRICULTURE, LIVESTOCK, MANUFACTURING, OR MINING, HACIENDAS RELIED UPON AN ORGANIZED LABOR FORCE AND COMMERCIAL SYSTEMS, AND PROSPERED BY PRODUCING A VARIETY OF PRODUCTS FROM SUGAR TO HENEQUÉN, GRAINS, TEQUILA AND PULQUE.

OPPOSITE: *The inviting steps at Hacienda Chimay are carpeted with the blooms of majestic flamboyan trees.*

ABOVE: *A handcarved stone basin-turned-aquatic garden of Hacienda Xcumpich.*

Designed for self-sufficiency, haciendas consisted typically of a *casa principal* (main house), chapel and an extensive arrangement of outbuildings and open spaces that included corrals, stables, barns, machine houses and/or processing structures, workers' quarters and workshops. Water tanks and stone aqueduct channels provided necessary water storage and a system of irrigation. Regional differences in climate, natural resources and construction elements contributed to the particular layout and appearance of each hacienda. From stone, adobe, and wood to earthen and mineral pigments, indigenous materials typically accompanied decorative ironwork, grand scale rooms, covered porches and courtyards to exude a physicality of permanence and grandeur. Following the Mexican Revolution, the landed estates began their passage into history as the feudal hacienda system was abolished and land reforms dramatically reduced the acreage of many haciendas.

OPPOSITE: *Standing as a testament to its working past, the Casa de Máquina reveals graceful architectural details. Hacienda Uayamón.*

RIGHT: *Contemporary stone spheres surround the original colonial wellhead at Hacienda El Alto, Morelia, Michoacán.*

ABOVE: *Hacienda Sodzil's graceful staircase creates an inviting atmosphere.*

Thanks to the efforts of pioneering architects, homeowners and preservationists that we showcased in our earlier books, including *The New Hacienda* and *Casa Yucatán*, the overall heightened interest in architectural preservation and adaptive reuse has fueled Mexico's burgeoning restoration movement in the last decade, catapulting restored haciendas and colonial homes into the international spotlight with their new extended lives as luxury hotels and unique homes. Nationals and foreigners alike are rescuing and reviving Mexico's architectural treasures, and sparking design inspiration throughout the world.

RIGHT: Old santos *are uniquely displayed on antique corbels at Suliram, Mérida.*

BELOW: In Mérida, Casa Santana's *unique collection of antiques and religious art blend beautifully with the restored home's colorful walls and patterned tiles.*

ABOVE: At *Casa Aurora,*
a richly painted bathroom
features a sink made from old
colonial, carved-stone elements.
Design by Manolo Vega.

OPPOSITE: A *sacred* ceiba
tree shares the bathroom suite
with guests at Hacienda San
José Cholul, Yucatán.

The design and essential architectural elements of the hacienda have withstood the rigors of time and have become an ever-increasing influence for architects and designers in the twenty-first-century world of home and commercial design. Though the feudal hacienda system of old is no longer operational in Mexico, its namesake is enjoying renewed attention in architectural design worldwide. Today, the word *hacienda* conjures up various images of Mexican-influenced rustic elegance, heralded in titles of upscale hotels, restaurants, ranch resorts, real estate developments, spas, and various businesses.

In our twenty-five years as antique dealers and designers, we have witnessed this evolution of the richly expressive hacienda style, specifically as it manifests in residential living spaces throughout Mexico and the U.S. Whether a country hacienda or colonial home, the term *hacienda* has become synonymous with a grand, old-world residence. Because Mexico's colonial period saw the construction of both rural haciendas and town houses simultaneously, these two building types share a variety of design and architectural characteristics. *Hacienda Style* consequently features both types of living spaces in order to elucidate variations of design we have seen within the hacienda style.

Our ongoing appreciation of Mexico's cultural richness has led us on a fascinating journey that has spawned eight design books and numerous design projects in the U.S. and Mexico, including an eighteenth-century Mexican hacienda restoration. We have traveled to the henequén estates of Yucatán and Campeche, the tequila haciendas of Jalisco, the grain estates in Puebla and the chocolate haciendas of Tabasco, visiting countless haciendas impressively restored to their original splendor. Extended visits to Mexico's vibrant colonial cities, including Mérida, Oaxaca and Morelia, have also greatly contributed to our research and it has been our delight to photograph the treasures whose architectural and design histories have so inspired our work.

OPPOSITE: *Hacienda La Pinka's front* portal *features rich traditional Yucatán colors and stone columns.*

PAGE 22: *The sala at Hacienda de los Santos in Alamos, Sonora, features an impressive display of antique crucifixes collected by owners Jim and Nancy Swickard throughout their extensive global travels.*

PAGE 23: *At Hacienda El Alto in Morelia, colonial treasures are displayed with ceramics and unique mineral specimens against ancient stone walls.*

A walk through a hacienda today illustrates the distinctive vocabulary of architectural elements, painted and tiled design, colors and natural materials that bespeak hacienda design and create the essence of the hacienda's strong character. Amidst tropical verdure, massive stone walls surround thick hardwood doors that open into a central courtyard, framed by stone columns supporting tall arcaded walkways. Centuries-old stone pavers encircle a quiet fountain, old *canales* (rainspouts) cast dramatic shadows on yellow ocher walls, and *marcos*, or stone surrounds carved in bas-relief, outline tall doors and windows. Wandering down palm-filled corridors, one glimpses views through doors to generously-proportioned rooms—as tall as they are wide—with rough hewn beams, chandeliers and richly colored walls. Underfoot, cool tiled floors beckon entrance, inviting a closer look at the time-worn patina of early colonial trunks and tables. At every turn, the timeless beauty of handcrafted wood, stone carved elements and stucco textures intrigue, and the aura of monastic austerity is palpable.

It is this rich imagery and time-honored character of the hacienda, and its newly restored forms, that were the inspiration for *Hacienda Style*. Today's innovative architects and designers working to honor and revive pre-Hispanic and colonial traditions amidst contemporary contexts continue to capture our interest. Their projects and vision have contributed to our own understanding of the richness of colonial restorations and the importance in connecting to the original elements that serve as soulful witness to a building's past.

Most recently, individual homeowners are translating the visual vocabulary of hacienda architecture and interior design into their own new or existing home construction projects. Accompanying this widespread movement is a heightened attraction to Mexico's natural building materials and antique architectural elements—doors, window guards, columns, beams, floor tile and unique artifacts—whose authenticity and sensual appeal embody an era of craftsmanship that contrasts sharply with our own.

In our work over the last two decades on various hacienda-style design projects, we have seen a strong interest from our homeowner clients in achieving authenticity with hacienda building designs, colors and materials. Through traveling directly to sites of interest, they are seeking hands-on familiarity with building details such as architectural ornament and scale of indoor-outdoor living spaces and courtyards.

Equipped with a knowledge rooted in old-world Mexican traditions, homeowners are better able to communicate their needs and desires to architects and builders. One California couple we accompanied to Mexico brought along their architect, builder and landscape designer. In between lunch design discussions at hacienda hotels, or an often-necessary afternoon dip in a water tank-turned-swimming pool, the tape measure was in constant use, measuring tall column heights, portal depths and rooflines.

Haciendas today, however, are not just subjects of residential revivals and inspiration for new home construction, but also unique travel destinations in themselves. In the last decade, as many haciendas have transitioned to luxe hotels and resorts, global travelers have become acquainted with the hacienda design aesthetic. Passing through old stone arches and witnessing the grandeur of 18-foot ceilings and secluded courtyards is not just happening vicariously via the pages of design books and magazines. Reincarnated in myriad other structures, the virtues of hacienda architecture and design are proliferating in both the private and public sector. Resorts, real estate developments, restaurants, retail stores and medical centers are drawing great inspiration from centuries-old haciendas of past eras.

In this volume, we hope to provide a visual framework for the key elements of hacienda design, while showcasing innovative ways in which hacienda elements can be creatively integrated in both new construction, and revived or re-adapted for restoration projects. We draw on our many years of research throughout Mexico, as well as our passion for finding and importing colonial furniture, antique doors, beams and roof tile for our clients. Our recent experience—incorporating many Mexican design elements into the building of our own hacienda home in Texas—has been especially rewarding and inspiring.

Thanks to the sensitive restoration efforts of owner Deborah LaChapelle, Casa Santana is resplendent with rich colorful wall textures that reveal varied layers of old paint. Original concrete tiles inspired the mustard-gold hue of the wainscot. Yucatán.

A trinity of skylights brings a heavenly glow to Hacienda Santa Cruz's restored chapel in the Yucatán. Restoration by owner Fiona St. Clair.

Yucatán Focus

In recent years, the Yucatán Peninsula has been a key center of hacienda restoration activity—which is why this volume gives special highlight to this region. The estates of Yucatán combine in their history the three great periods of ancient Yucatán: the pre-Columbian period, the era of Spanish rule, and the henequén boom years of the late nineteenth and early twentieth centuries. With an extremely high concentration—approximately four hundred—of haciendas spanning a wide range of architectural styles, the Yucatán offers a rich tapestry from which to study and showcase the evolution and stylistic details of haciendas. The region, more than any other in Mexico at this time, has attracted innovative individuals and a variety of organizations who have adapted Mexico's monuments of the past into myriad new uses, including hotels, restaurants, museums, cultural centers and artist workshops.

Many dedicated preservationists and talented Mexican design professionals, including architect Salvador Reyes Ríos and designer Josefina Larraín, have been responsible for reawakening old traditions and spawning contemporary adaptations respecting the diversity of their clients' purposes. Through his collaborative work with Grupo Plan's hacienda projects as associate architect, Reyes Ríos honed his appreciation for colonial restoration and developed his design style for both restored and modern constructions. In *Casa Yucatán*, we showcased many of the couple's restoration and design projects and we proudly feature their most recent projects in this volume. Our research and travels have been greatly enriched by Reyes Ríos' and Larraín's expertise and passionate knowledge of Yucatán design.

OPPOSITE: *Yucatán's old haciendas are rich with architectural ornament and colonial grandeur. Hacienda Santa Rosa, Yucatán.*

BELOW: *Rich stone textures are abundant in both old haciendas and contemporary homes. At Casa Barrera in Mérida, a local, natural stone is elevated to artful sculpture.*

One of Mexico's leading preservation pioneers, Roberto Hernández and his company, Grupo Plan, has also been at the forefront in preserving Mexico's rich cultural heritage through hacienda revivals in Yucatán and Campeche. Under the direction of head architect Luis Bosoms, haciendas and colonial buildings have been rescued and artfully restored to their original splendor as modern-day luxury hotels. Starting in the mid '90s, Grupo Plan has completed restoration work on the following haciendas—Temozón, Ochil, Santa Rosa, San José Cholul, Hacienda Uayamón, Hacienda Chichí de los Lagos, Hacienda Itzincab Cámara and Hacienda Puerta Campeche. Currently, three other Yucatán projects are underway.

Preservation efforts by Hernández and others are intended not only to revive living spaces or foster tourist venues, but also to breathe new life into the communities that surround the hacienda. For more than a decade, Hernández and wife Claudia Madrazo have been tireless in their dedication to the social and cultural development of the Mayan region and its people. Together they founded Haciendas del Mundo Maya, A.C. Foundation, whose motto in Maya is N*aat*-H*a*, meaning "Learn About and Understand to Transform." For over ten years, the foundation, headed by Marilu Hernández, has increased employment through the development and implementation of community projects that revolve around rich cultural traditions such as handcrafts and textile production. Roberto Hernández's part in the hacienda movement has been a clear and vital contribution to preserving this area's valuable history, bringing recognition to this rich Yucatán heritage for future generations.

ABOVE: *At Los Dos in the Yucatán, owners David Sterling and Keith Heitke added a dramatic and inviting swimming pool during the home's restoration.*

ABOVE: At *Hacienda Puerta Campeche* a series of pool rooms connect through open doorways to sun-filled roofless rooms that open onto gardens.

Hacienda Puerta Campeche, an elegant hotel in the historic heart of Campeche, was artfully restored by Grupo Plan under the direction of architect Luis Bosoms. A series of seventeenth-century houses, the estate features impressive water spaces accompanied by colonial architecture. Inside the cool, shadowy presence of ancient stone walls, one can float through a series of pool "rooms" that connect through open doorways then out into sun-filled, roofless rooms that open onto tropical gardens. White hammocks strung the width of the room and skimming the surface of the turquoise water contrast sharply with deep yellow-hued walls and high wood-beamed ceilings.

THIS PAGE: *Hammocks skim the water's surface in the shadowy, seventeenth-century rooms at Hacienda Puerta Campeche, a luxury hotel in historical downtown Campeche.*

In Mérida, Casa Colonial features an elegant, arcaded portal, pool and guest rooms added to the home's back courtyard during restoration. Design by Phillipe and Dominique Duneton.

In presenting idea-filled examples of authentic hacienda design, *Hacienda Style* hopes to inspire you to bring the hacienda style back home to your projects—be they in the U.S. or abroad. Our in-depth research into the details and materials that transition well to new construction in the U.S. inspire many of this book's chapters, including "Cocinas" and "Color & Stencils," which highlights traditional Mexican paint colors and the use of decorative wall stencils. An extension of our seven other books that explore Mexican architecture, antiques and hacienda design—*Mexican Country Style, The New Hacienda, Casa Adobe, Adobe Details, Casa Yucatán, Mexican Details* and *Hacienda Courtyards*—*Hacienda Style* continues the celebration of the rich hacienda design style that is flourishing in the U.S. and beyond.

OPPOSITE: An elegant swimming pool and fountain are the central focus of Casa Arroyo Veloz's courtyard. Architect, Henry Ponce.

BELOW: This inviting pool fountain is masterfully chinked with beautiful local limestone. Casa Carolina Cárdenas, Mérida, Yucatán.

Arquitectura

DISTINCT ARCHITECTURAL ELEMENTS INSIDE AND OUT CREATE THE ESSENCE OF HACIENDA CHARACTER—IMPOSING ENTRANCE ARCHES AND COLUMNS, THICK STUCCOED MASONRY WALLS, MASSIVE CEILING BEAMS AND CORBELS, OLD FLOORING, IRON WINDOW GRILLES AND WOODEN DOORS SURROUNDED BY CARVED STONE MARCOS (FRAMES). Whether one is restoring the original elements for reuse in a colonial hacienda or home, or integrating antique elements into a new hacienda-style home, the inclusion of these features offers a tangible link to the rich heritage of Mexico's traditional construction techniques and their various regional differences.

Because the haciendas and colonial homes in Mexico were built over a span of three centuries, their diverse architectural styles reflect the style in vogue at the time they were built, along with geographical location, availability of local building materials and the personal tastes of owners. Many common design elements—from columns, arches, doors and flooring—were shared by colonial homes and rural haciendas during Mexico's colonial period, which is why both types of buildings appear in this architectural chapter.

◆◆◆◆◆◆◆◆◆◆◆

OPPOSITE: *Elegant stone columns support an arcaded portal at Hacienda San José Cholul, Yucatán.*

ABOVE: *A Moorish design influence is visible in this Yucatán colonial hacienda entrance arch.*

PAGE 38: *Top, Hacienda La Luz, Tabasco. Bottom right: Hacienda San Antonio Cucul, Mérida, Yucatán.*

PAGE 39: *Bottom, Hacienda San Pedro Chukuaxin.*

ABOVE: *In the Yucatán, rich architectural ornament adds decorative interest to old colonial haciendas. Hacienda Sodzil, Mérida.*

OPPOSITE: *Hacienda Santa Rosa's arcaded portal features stately arches and an elegant frieze pattern.*

During the later Porfiriato period (1876–1911, marked by the reign of Mexico President Porfirio Díaz), heightened interest in lavish architectural expressions and preferences for neoclassical and eclectic ornamentation became prevalent in both city homes and rural estates.

The structural vitality of many old haciendas remains strong today, as defensive measures such as high perimeter walls, observation towers and heavy nail-studded doors were crafted to withstand centuries of use. The kind of structural details and outbuildings seen upon any one estate varied according to the estate's operations: granaries or barns for agricultural use; fermenting sheds for tequila or pulque production; and smelting rooms for silver operations. At the many ex-cattle and henequén haciendas we photographed in the Yucatán, features such as stone aqueducts, feeding troughs, cisterns and water tanks punctuated the landscape, topped by towering chimneys once linked to machine houses.

ABOVE: An intricately carved stone marco (frame) adds decorative interest to the doors at Hacienda Yodzonot.

OPPOSITE: The warmth of orange-hued Ticul stone tile creates an inviting atmosphere at the front portal of Hacienda Yodzonot's guesthouse.

Early cattle haciendas were typically single story with a tall roof parapet and fronted by arches and columns. Carved stone rainspouts, or *canales*, protruded from parapet facades to provide efficient rainwater removal. Early roofs were supported with large round or square *vigas* (wooden beams) and *mensulas* (corbels). Iron beams, imported from Belgium mainly in the nineteenth century, also made their way into colonial homes and haciendas.

LEFT: At *Hacienda Itzincab Cámara many of the doors feature small window openings for increased ventilation and light. Simple wrought-iron grilles add protection.*

OPPOSITE: A *traditional* alacena (*wall cabinet*) *is fronted by colonial doors with iron* clavos. *Owner's suite at Hacienda Temozón, Yucatán.*

Today, many of these beamed ceilings are being updated for increased light with the addition of skylights that anchor the end of each room. High windows, referred to as *oculos* (round or oval shaped wall openings), are also important elements that offer additional light and ventilation between rooms. Old beams and corbels are being newly positioned for decorative use above kitchen counters or put to use as fireplace mantels. Others are fashioned into thick planks for long dining tables.

44

THIS PAGE: At *Hacienda*
Santa Rosa, richly patterned
stencils were re-created from
original patterns.

OPPOSITE: *Tall doors and*
shuttered windows accentuate
Hacienda La Pinka's high
ceilings and elegantly painted
walls. A colonial santo rests
on a table supported by carved
columns from Michoacán.

Carved as round, tapered and square, early colonial stone columns
gave elegant support to long, arcaded portales. Often not reaching above
eight feet, it was not until the Porfiriato that height spans generally
increased for arches, columns, doors and windows. This period of lavish
architectural embellishment brought additional decorative details,
including cornices and friezes, to rural haciendas and colonial homes.
Also adorning the inner arches of prominent buildings of this time,
almoadillado, or decorative raised stucco, has been beautifully restored at
Hacienda Chichí de los Lagos in the Yucatán.

LEFT: At Hacienda Itzincab Cámara, a recessed interior head of a window, called derrame, accentuates thick stone walls. Yucatán.

BELOW: Antique sugar molds posture next to Mexican raised-paneled doors. Home of the authors, Joe P. Carr and Karen Witynski, Hacienda Granada, Texas.

OPPOSITE: An old pair of Yucatán doors feature small window openings that open for increased ventilation and light.

The massive doors of haciendas, churches and important colonial buildings radiate a compelling sense of history and readily define the importance of the building with their hand-adzed rich hardwoods and decorative iron details. Mortise and tenon construction featured thick planks, wrought-iron *clavos* (hand-forged nails), corner braces and hinges.

With so many regional differences, there is a seemingly endless variety of doors that can be seen in Mexico. Simple, flat plank styles were commonly found on hacienda workshop buildings or storehouses. *Tableros* (raised panel doors that featured intricate carvings) were often used in prominent buildings, including haciendas and colonial homes. In tropical regions such as the Yucatán and Campeche, tops of doors were designed with hinged shutters for increased ventilation. Referred to as *ventanillas* (small windows), these hinged openings are commonly seen in a simple, pointed arch motif with iron grilles covering their exterior.

The baroque-inspired *capialzado* (conical-shaped, sculpted ornament that appears over the exterior head of doors and windows) is commonly painted to contrast with exterior walls. Inside, the interior head of windows and doors is recessed in a concave, semicircular shape, called *derrame*, which beautifully accentuates thick stone walls. At Hacienda San Antonio Cucul in the Yucatán, the kitchen window's derrame is painted a striking blue in contrast to white walls, highlighting its artful shape.

LEFT: *Clay roof tiles mix well with chinked stone walls, Ticul-stone molding and elegant carved columns.*

OPPOSITE: *Raised-panel colonial doors anchor a glass entrance to this Yucatán home. A large skylight brings natural light to a stone tile and pebble floor.*

As haciendas were designed with fortification in mind, windows were predominately constructed as tall, door-like openings, in the same height and width as the building's existing doorways. They were covered with solid door-shutters that opened to interiors for light and ventilation, with iron or wood grilles protecting exteriors. Fine examples of turned wooden spindle grilles can be seen in old construction, for example at Hacienda La Gavia in the state of Mexico and Hacienda Chichí de los Lagos in the Yucatán. The French influence during the Porfiriato period prompted the design of highly ornate window grilles and balustrades.

THIS PAGE: *The inviting entrance of this hacienda-style home features rich color and a colonial bench. A handcrafted door features wrought-iron clavos, Joe P. Carr Design.*

ABOVE: *The impressive
entrance to Casa Aurora in
the Yucatán features thick,
massive walls, a wrought-iron
arched gate and stone pavers.
Design by Manolo Vega.*

Throughout Mexico, prominent flooring choices included stone, brick, clay tile and concrete tile. In regions with access to forested areas, wood plank floors were seen; however, wood flooring was not common in Yucatán haciendas. Rough-cut stone remains popular for outdoor spaces and patios. Polished stone tile, especially the Yucatán's orange-hued Ticul stone and white macedonia, are favored for portales and interiors.

Many haciendas and old town homes still feature their original, patterned cement tiles (*mosaicos de pasta*). Originating in France and Spain, these tiles traveled to Mexico on ships that carried them as ballast along with marble and clay roof tiles. Offering a cool, colorful surface—especially ideal in warm climates—concrete floor tiles were produced in myriad colors and patterns, providing rooms with an elegant, colorful design statement without overdecoration.

Thanks to both the tile-making technology imported from Europe and pioneering individuals in Mexico who are dedicated to preserving this art, high-quality concrete tiles continue to be made in Mexico today. With old buildings, the original tiles are not always found in good condition. In this case, the intact tiles are salvaged and often placed in a floor's center, surrounded by a polished cement border that frames the original tiles. Patterned concrete tiles are also being used as colorful wainscots, especially in small spaces. Many old tiles showing decades of wear are becoming textural accents for shower niches or kitchen counters and islands. Today, the popularity of colorful concrete tiles has spread to the U.S. and homeowners and architects are enjoying the infinite design options they offer.

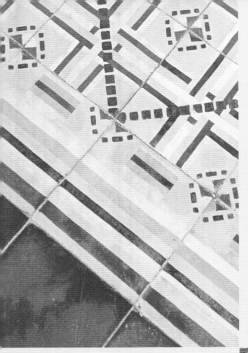

Wall *nichos*, commonly found in hacienda chapels for display of religious *santos*, have now become popular in hallways, kitchens and dining rooms. In addition to holding religious objects, they are also home to contemporary sculptures, colorful baskets, glasses and dishes. Sometimes they are simply artful showcases for old antique tile. *Alacenas* (built-in wall cabinets), traditionally found in hacienda kitchens and dining rooms, today continue to offer convenient storage and are being designed into myriad rooms as a unique showcase for antique doors.

PREVIOUS PAGE: *Original concrete tiles are surrounded by a polished concrete border. Restoration and design by architect Salvador Reyes Ríos and designer Josefina Larraín, Casa Reyes-Larraín. Mérida.*

ABOVE AND OPPOSITE: *From floral to bold geometric patterns, concrete floor tiles are available in many designs.*

THIS PAGE: *Restored to its original colonial charm, Hotel Casona de Tita in Oaxaca is rich with unique architectural details and local materials.*

OPPOSITE: *At Casa Aurora, a grand-scale* sala *features a beamed ceiling with skylights. Custom colored floor tiles and richly painted walls create an inviting atmosphere. Design by Manolo Vega, Yucatán.*

Interior walls were painted with traditional *cal*, or lime-based paint, favored because it bonds well to lime stucco and allows stone walls to breathe. The addition of colorful wainscots and decorative *cenefas* (stencils) elevates walls to become their own decorative statement. The use of paint color as decoration is detailed in our "Color & Stencils" chapter.

OPPOSITE: *In the Yucatán, an arcaded portal is supported by old colonial stone columns. Hacienda Itzincab Cámara.*

THIS PAGE: *Painted beams and stenciled walls complement natural wood doors and floors. Hacienda Itzincab Cámara.*

At Hacienda Yodzonot in the Yucatán, the rich textures of old stone create a bold and inviting statement. Limestone rocks artfully surround the entrance to the kitchen.

Color & Stencils

FOR CENTURIES, COLOR HAS PLAYED A VITAL ROLE IN MEXICAN ARCHITECTURE.

FROM THE BOLDLY PAINTED PYRAMIDS AND MURALS OF THE PRE-HISPANIC

CIVILIZATIONS TO THE NOBLE HOMES AND HACIENDAS OF THE SPANISH

COLONIAL ERA, MEXICO'S TRADITIONAL COLORS HAVE A RICH LEGACY.

With origins in earthen, mineral and vegetal sources, Mexico's indigenous

colorants combined with *cal*, or lime paint, to produce a variety of vibrant colors,

including deep rusty reds and yellow ochers that range in tone from bright yellow

to burnt orange. Throughout Mexico, these colors and their subtle variations were

the most popular exterior hacienda colors.

A deep, earthen red called *rojo hacienda*, or hacienda red as it's referred to in

Mexico, on a colonial entrance arch attracts with the warmth it exudes. Combined with

the matte finish, the color evokes the sense that it has witnessed time's passage.

A pure white—from calcite found in limestone—was favored for exterior

accents and interior walls. Green, most often in jade-like tones, adorned early

eighteenth-century doors and wooden elements.

◆◆◆◆◆◆◆◆◆◆

OPPOSITE: *Rich color, elegant stencils and patterned concrete floor tile lend a regal air to the rooms at Hacienda Chenché de las Torres.*

ABOVE: *An intricate lace-like stencil pattern tops a colorful wainscot, Hacienda Chenché de las Torres, Yucatán.*

Maya blue—a rare clay organic complex created by the early Maya civilization—was used to decorate murals, ceramics and art objects from the pre-Columbian era to the colonial period and into the nineteenth century. Derived from indigo and a special white clay found in the Sacalum region of the Yucatán, this alluring blue was used in colonial paintings and architecture throughout the Yucatán Peninsula. Maya blue was so highly coveted that it became a valuable export to other regions, including Cuba, the Caribbean and Mexico's gulf coast. According to Dr. Miguel José Yacamán, who has extensively studied the origins of Maya blue, the range of tones—from bright blue to violet blue—were derived from the formation of nanoparticles inside the clay when heated.

Since the sixteenth century, the entire colonial city of Izamal, including its renowned convent, has been awash in tones of bright yellow ocher trimmed in crisp white. This widely recognized yellow has become a favored tone for haciendas and colonial-style homes, even garden walls, and has come to be known as Izamal yellow.

The intoxicating vibrancy of Mexico's traditional colors is multiplied thanks to the scale of hacienda structures and their unique architectural characteristics: towering walls topped with merlons, decorative cornices, friezes and raised stucco embellishments. Aged walls featuring *rajueleado*, a traditional method using a repetition of chinked stones to punctuate a stuccoed wall, are mesmerizing in rich color.

Inside, eighteen-foot-high walls are defined and dressed up with a variety of old-world hand-painted designs and details, including wainscots crowned with regal bands of decorative *cenefas*, or stencils. Even hefty wooden ceiling beams and nail-studded doors become an alluring canvas for Mexico's paint colors. When contrasting colors are used for interior nichos and derrames, and *capialzados* (conical ornament over exterior head of doors and windows), color can truly exert its power upon architectural details.

An inviting bathroom at Hacienda Puerta Campeche features bold color, natural textures accentuated, and dramatic shadows created by wooden beams and skylights.

The violet-blue arcaded facade of Hacienda Santa Rosa dazzles with its crisp white outlines and elegant, geometric frieze pattern in red and yellow. Beneath its graceful arches, two thin blue bands, each paired with a stencil flourish, run horizontally along light yellow walls. Above, in close proximity to the hefty wooden ceiling beams, a wider band envelops an ornate European-inspired stencil that encircles the open-air portal.

Many of today's restoration projects are undergoing faithful replication of original details including wall and door colors, as well as any original stencil work. On numerous occasions throughout our hacienda explorations and design work, we would diligently scrape away a section of a wall's outer layer to discover hints of color from past eras. Spurred by this passion for uncovering the vibrant palette of Mexico's centuries-old hacienda colors, coupled with the rising interest from U.S. homeowners/designers in obtaining authentic paint colors from this area, we worked together with Pittsburgh® Paints color lab to research and replicate these traditional hacienda colors. Our goal is to celebrate and spread the hues of old Mexico into new markets and contemporary living spaces through our exclusive Hacienda Style Color Palette from Pittsburgh® Paints.

Inviting color, colonial-style concrete tiles and handcrafted accents create soothing rooms at Hotel Marionetas, Mérida. Restoration and design by Dan and Sofi Bosco.

ABOVE: *Elegant stencil patterns punctuate this colorful wainscot for decorative interest.*

OPPOSITE: *Colorful walls and stencils artfully blend with patterned concrete tile and antiques at Suliram, Mérida, Yucatán. Designer, Raymond Branham.*

Decorative Use of Paint

In Colonial homes and haciendas especially, paint is a powerful tool in moderating a room's scale and easing original proportions to allow a new perception of space. In addition, the breadth and height of walls allow for myriad decorative painted effects.

Paint visually alters high-ceilinged rooms to create more intimacy: the ceiling color (most often white) can be extended down the wall to meet the main wall color. At this intersection, a thin defining line (in a different color) is used between the two colors. In essence, paint lowers the ceiling to give the room a more human scale. Another solution for adding intimacy and old-world style to tall rooms is to simulate with paint the effects of vigas, or ceiling beams. The painted ceiling stripes are often paired with real wooden corbels (painted the same color) that join the striped "beams" to the wall. The overall effect serves as a soothing completion to the room, and lessens its cavernous impression.

Further down the wall, the use of painted horizontal bands is a cue taken from the geometry of ceiling beams. Pioneered by architect Salvador Reyes Ríos and designer Josefina Larraín in their hacienda restorations, this technique creates a bold geometric statement and counterbalances a room's height. The Casa de Máquina of Hacienda Sacchich features a beautiful display of this technique in its guest bedrooms and adjoining bathrooms (featured in the chapter on Restored Haciendas, p. 130). On the opposite plane, vertical bands of color also work beautifully in similar high-ceilinged spaces, as evidenced by the inviting light yellow stripes that rise up against white walls in Hacienda Xcumpich's elegant library.

Wainscots, or *rodapíes*, are a traditional solution in separating the color change between floor and wall. Most often seen as a solid band of accent color, three to four feet in height, variations include solid bands topped with thinner, same-color bands, as seen at Hacienda San José Cholul, or multiple bands of varying colors as seen at Hacienda Itzincab. In some restoration projects, wall colors often find their inspiration in the palette of a room's original floor tiles. The deep red and gray concrete tiles at Hacienda Xcumpich, for example, prompted the choice of rich red walls and an elegant gray wainscot defined with white stripes.

Colorful bands create a bold wainscot that echoes the linear design of the concrete floor tiles. Tall beamed ceilings and doors lend the room a luxurious air. Hacienda San José Cholul, Yucatán.

Smaller spaces can be amplified by flowing the floor color up the wall, either via paint or tile. A painted wainscot achieves this effect in either a low one-foot height or traditional three- to four-foot height. In the case of tile floors, using a similar color tile as wall trim in two rows versus the usual one row increases the widening effect. Both of these applications have been well-utilized by Reyes Ríos and Larraín in their colonial restoration projects.

Hand-Painted Designs & Stencils

Hand-painted decorative designs have long adorned Mexican churches, convents, prominent homes and haciendas. European decorative painting styles, as well as individual artists' tastes, created vogues in painted wall design varying with the time period of the structure. Floral designs, urns and pastoral garden-scene murals were prevalent, as were elegant fleur-de-lis motifs.

At Hacienda Chichí de los Lagos, the original hand-painted flowering vines surrounding principal doors and windows were beautifully restored by Grupo Plan and their architectural team, headed by architect Luis Bosoms. At Hacienda San José Cholul, another Grupo Plan restoration project, the original, delicate hand-painted designs are still visible on the chapel's walls.

OPPOSITE: *Restored colonial stencils surround a wooden window grille and chapel doorway at Hacienda Chichi de los Lagos, Yucatán.*

THIS PAGE: *This colonial Yucatán convent wall features centuries-old hand-painted decorative designs.*

LEFT: *Rich color and intricate stencils envelop the charming chapel at Hacienda Itzincab Cámara, Yucatán.*

OPPOSITE: *In this regal bedroom, twenty-foot ceilings create an ideal backdrop for rich paint color and stencil patterns. Design by Raymond Branham. Suliram, Mérida.*

FOLLOWING SPREAD: *Beautiful stencils adorn the walls at Hacienda Santa Rosa.*

Stencils, or cenefas, added wall decoration through the use of a template and repetitive paint stamping process. Though repeating floor-to-ceiling patterns occur, most frequently stencils appeared atop colorful wainscots (*rodapié de cenefa*) and near the wall-ceiling border (*frisos de cenefas*). Designs hailing from France and Spain were prominent in stencil work in the Yucatán during the late nineteenth century—or Porfiriato Period (1876–1911)—when trade and imports of European goods were at a peak in this region of Mexico. French construction materials (including roof tile and cement floor tiles) were especially in demand, resulting in a prevalence of French-inspired stencil decoration coming to the Yucatán.

It was while researching *Casa Yucatán* that we became intrigued by the vast variety of floral and geometric stencil patterns used in Yucatán haciendas. Original stencil designs, mostly French in origin, impressively spanned walls from floor to ceiling at Hacienda San Antonio Millet and Hacienda Itzincab. One visit to Hacienda Chunchucmil—pre-restoration—revealed multiple spaces with highly ornate hand-painted designs and stencils, including one room with unique Oriental motifs. At Hacienda Chenché de las Torres, we delighted in photographing the exquisite stencil work in the casa principal, especially the intricate white lace-like patterns encircling the rich blue walls of the grand scale drawing room.

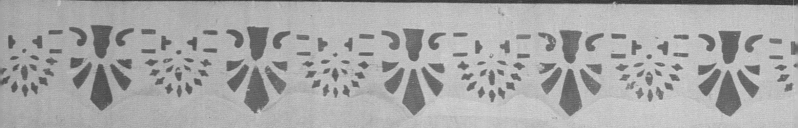

Another fine example of the use of stencils to enrich and unify interiors is seen at Suliram, a colonial-style home in downtown Mérida. Artist/designer Raymond Branham found inspiration in old Victorian stencil designs which he replicated for use throughout his grand-scale, two-story residence. For the long, arcaded hallways and various open-air sitting rooms, Branham chose a turquoise blue tone for the wainscot and stencil pattern that provides a colorful contrast to his colonial paintings and wrought-iron hanging lanterns. An elegant four-poster bed in a guest room is surrounded by terra-cotta and pistachio-hued stenciled walls, adding to the room's old-world sophistication.

PREVIOUS SPREAD: *Hacienda Itzincab Cámara's casa principal is enveloped by beautiful restored stencils.*

THIS PAGE: *On the portal at Los Dos, a hammock rests above a beautiful wall stencil. Mérida, Yucatán.*

OPPOSITE: *A grey-hued wainscot, colorful walls and original floor tiles enhance this art-filled room at Hacienda Xcumpich, Yucatán.*

In addition to inscribing new walls with decorative interest, old stencil designs stand witness to past eras. Today's architects and restoration specialists now highlight sections of old painted walls, often with a simple outline, to frame them for new generations to enjoy.

ABOVE AND RIGHT:
European-inspired stencils
accentuate the tall, beamed
ceilings at Hacienda Santa
Rosa, Yucatán.

OPPOSITE: *Hacienda Santa*
Rosa's grand-scale portal
features two colorful bands
accented by stencil patterns.

84

Cocinas

AGAINST A BACKDROP OF LUSTROUS HAND-PAINTED TILES AND WOOD-BEAMED CEILINGS, A MEXICAN HACIENDA KITCHEN SIMMERED WITH PUNGENT AROMAS, CONVERSATION, AND ACTIVITY FROM AN EARLY HOUR.

Typically spacious, well-stocked, and laden with cherished, well-worn implements, colonial hacienda *cocinas* were inspired by centuries-old convent kitchens charged with preparing meals for hundreds. Along its walls, upon its long countertops and central islands, inside space-saving nichos, alacenas, and *trasteros*, the hands and tools that worked the drama of kitchen life played out daily.

As this description of a Mexican kitchen from Adela Fernández's book, *Traditional Mexican Cooking*, testifies, the actual foods that propelled these preparations were in no small variety or supply:

The pantry, crammed with great baskets and jars of salt, sugar, *pinole*, corn, chickpeas, lentils and coffee, tubs full of lard, numerous tortilla baskets, chilies of all varieties, herbs and other condiments, nets stuffed with roselle flower and tamarind . . . suspended from the ceiling were cheeses wrapped in muslin, jars of honey, great bottles

◆◆◆◆◆◆◆◆◆

OPPOSITE: *The spacious kitchen at Hacienda San Gabriel de las Palmas is anchored by a tiled island that houses multiple burners.*

ABOVE: *An old Mexican ceramic features handpainted floral designs. Collection of the authors, Joe P. Carr and Karen Witynski. Hacienda Granada, Texas.*

of oil, vinegar, wine and brandy. Stacked on board were blocks of raw brown sugar and chocolate wrapped in corn husks. Hanging from ropes were spicy sausages such as *longaniza*, red and green *chorizo*, salted meat and strings of garlic . . .

ABOVE: *For centuries, the stone three-legged* metate *has been a staple implement in Mexican kitchens.*

RIGHT: *A masterful design of Talavera tiles adorn the walls and countertop of this colonial kitchen in Puebla.*

OPPOSITE: *Built in the sixteenth century, Puebla's Convento de Santa Rosa is resplendent with Talavera tiles, nichos, wooden spoon racks and glazed pottery.*

OPPOSITE BOTTOM: *An antique Mexican spoon rack holds wooden chocolate whisks. Hacienda Granada, Texas.*

Though today's kitchens no longer require endless hours for grinding, chopping and rolling food ingredients; wood to feed stovetop burners; or adobe or stone ovens to bake bread, the original designs and style of early colonial hacienda kitchens remain integral to kitchen function in contemporary building. *Cocinas Mexicanas* and, increasingly, their counterparts in America, combine familiar old-world elements with modern fixtures and appliances: hand-painted Talavera tiles, stencils, rustic tables and chairs, simple iron chandeliers and traditional utilitarian objects surround modern stovetops and polished concrete surfaces. For modern day homebuilders eager to bring authenticity to their own designs, the age-old beauty of the early colonial kitchen's furnishings, implements and storage solutions offer a wealth of inspiration.

Usually filled with locally-made ceramic plates and cups, the trastero, or freestanding cupboard, is a ubiquitous kitchen piece. Often brightly painted, its top shelves were either open or covered by spindled or slatted doors. Similar in design to the trastero, the *aguadera* has a deeper

RIGHT: *The traditional Talavera tile island serves as center stage during cooking classes at Los Dos, Mérida.*

OPPOSITE: *The inviting kitchen at Los Dos features a soaring stove hood, stencil designs and a split-level island that houses both a sink and dishwasher. Colonial-style concrete floor tiles blend with Talavera tiles for a dramatic statement. Restoration and design by owners David Sterling and Keith Heitke.*

bottom shelf carved with round indentations or cutouts for holding ceramic water vessels. Adorning white-washed walls were *repisas*, or hanging shelves, often embellished with scalloped molding or decorative crests. Salvaged from the tops of trasteros, old *copetés*, or crests, can function as elegant racks from which to hang spoons, spatulas and ladles.

OPPOSITE: The island at Hacienda Granada is resplendent with traditional blue, white and yellow Talavera tiles. Design by authors Karen Witynski and Joe P. Carr.

THIS PAGE: A Mexican aguadera holds everyday kitchen items, large water ollas and old Guatemalan pitchers. Collection of the authors, Joe P. Carr and Karen Witynski. Hacienda Granada, Texas.

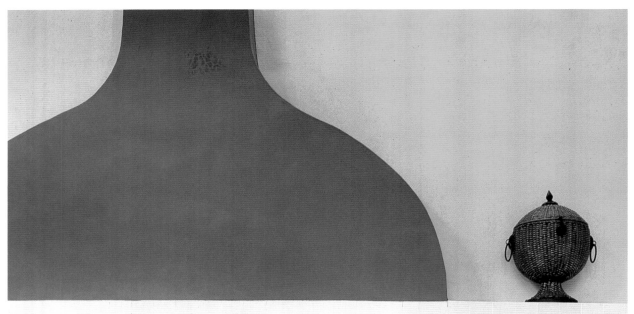

A traditional kitchen's working tools reflect the Mexican diet's focus on chilies and spices, and the ritual of tortilla making and sauce preparation. Spice grinding was accomplished with handcarved metates, the three-legged, pre-Hispanic flat grinding stones made of volcanic rock, and *molcajetes*, or small round stone mortars. Wooden *bateas*, or dough bowls, tortilla presses and *comals* (clay griddles) were indispensable in daily meal preparations. Ladles, *molinillos*, or chocolate whisks, sugar molds and grain-measure boxes were staple implements. Dried gourds were also a versatile kitchen aid. Large ones were hollowed out and used to keep tortillas warm, or perforated to function as colanders. Smaller gourds served as *jícaras*, or gourd cups, when cut in half.

Baskets abound in all shapes and sizes, handwoven in a variety of fibers including palm or henequén. Mexican *morteros* (or mortars), the large, sculptural wooden vessels once used to grind grain or coffee, hold kitchen supplies or fresh produce. Ceramics in every style imaginable—from open-handled dishes to serving platters—are displayed on shelves and hung on walls. Miniature glazed pots, often numbering in the hundreds, are hung over doorways and along walls to create ribbon-like displays. Circling the table or kitchen's perimeter are long benches, chairs, and low three-legged stools, offering respite and rest amidst the daily labors of kitchen life.

Nowhere inside the grand colonial homes or haciendas were beautifully patterned *azulejos* (tiles) more prominently used than the kitchen. Placed on almost every surface—walls, countertops and nichos—glazed tiles also accented the interwoven designs of clay brick floors. In the colonial Santa Rosa Convent in Puebla, the birthplace of the famed *mole poblano*, the entire cocina interior, including the vaulted ceiling, is enlivened with traditional blue, white and yellow Talavera tiles. Today, Mexican style kitchens feature colonial traditions with a contemporary twist: hand-painted tiles are innovatively mixed to create dramatic patterns on countertops and islands in beautiful contrast with colorful, polished concrete counters.

OPPOSITE: *A rich yellow polished-concrete countertop is enlivened by traditional Talavera-style tiles and a stove hood at Merimo Nah in Mérida. Design by architect Salvador Reyes Ríos and designer Josefina Larraín.*

ABOVE: *Traditional blue, white and yellow tiles create a beautiful backsplash at Merimo Nah, Yucatán.*

The type of Mexican tables seen commanding the center space of old-world kitchens are often crafted from cedar, mesquite or *sabino* (Mexican cypress) with open mortise and tenon construction, featuring simple plank tops and sturdy A-frame bases. Other popular styles include those with a decorative *faldon*, or apron, and a heavy, turned leg base that was often painted, as seen in the bright blue table at Hacienda Tecajete in Hidalgo.

If not dedicated to a rustic wooden table, the center of a hacienda kitchen featured a rectangular or semicircular tiled island, as well as a long countertop usually running the length of one wall. In ample kitchen spaces, the semicircular island shape becomes a wonderful curved canvas for showcasing tile, repetitious stencil designs or a polished concrete finish. The kitchens of Hacienda San Gabriel de las Palmas and Hacienda San Pedro Ovando feature fine examples of tiled, semicircular islands—inset with their original multiple burners.

Tiled countertops are a common feature in the layout of a colonial style kitchen. Depending on the length of the countertop, one, two or more arched openings punctuate the front and shelter shelves of large baskets or ceramics. Sinks and modern stovetops positioned above the arches allow easy installation and maintenance access (ovens are usually placed on an adjacent wall or integrated into central islands). The solidity of natural carved-stone sinks, especially in earthy orange and red tones, adds interest and contrast to concrete countertops.

Whether used as work space, eating area or both, many of today's kitchen islands have become highly functional with the addition of innovative, built-in features. Shelves and drawers increase storage on an island's ends, and cutting boards incorporate well into concrete tops. In designing our own hacienda-style kitchen in Texas, we inset a downdraft range in the tiled island's center and surrounded the semicircle with wood stools to create a dramatic exhibition-style working and seating area.

The restoration and design projects of architect Salvador Reyes Ríos and designer Josefina Larraín celebrate the integration of traditional colonial-style elements into functional contemporary spaces. Many of their kitchen projects are designed with efficient islands, elegant stove hoods or large arched nichos that beautifully anchor spaces. Smoothly polished, colored concrete counter and island surfaces often feature inset sinks and tiled accents on lateral surfaces. Recessed spaces below counters invite feet to nestle comfortably while standing, or provide room for chairs to be pulled up to the counter.

OPPOSITE: *An old Mexican ranch table and a shelf with large corbels add warmth to the colorfully-tiled kitchen at La Casa del Pocito, Mérida.*

ABOVE: *Colorful and exotic, the* pitahaya *is a favorite fruit in the Yucatán.*

PAGE 100: *Restored by artist/designer Raymond Branham, Suliram features a tile counter supported by wooden balustrades that were found treasures. Stencils and stained glass details create an elegant atmosphere.*

PAGE 101: *In the Yucatán, Hacienda Sotuta de Péon's original geometric concrete tile blends well with the ceramic counter tiles.*

At Los Dos, a restored colonial home and cooking school in Mérida, Yucatán, the inviting kitchen island designed by owners David Sterling and Keith Heitke features a masterful mix of tile patterns and houses both sink and dishwasher in a split-level design. The result is a convenient counter height for chopping and prepping foods, as well as a slightly lower level for seating. Above the island, a custom-designed, iron

pot rack keeps 20-plus pots and pans within easy reach, a traditional arrangement in the Mexican kitchen. Above-counter kitchen cabinets are seldom seen in colonial style design. Open shelves, either standing or hanging, antique furniture, or alacenas (wall cabinets fronted by wooden doors) are the storage choices most desired when replicating an authentic Mexican kitchen. If extra storage space is required, separate, walk-in pantries can be designed adjacent to the main kitchen space.

The massive yet often shapely stove hood is a unique design element found in large colonial homes and haciendas. In the Yucatán, the original kitchens of Hacienda Chunchucmil and Hacienda Temozón featured fine examples of venting hoods. At Hacienda San José del Refugio, a unique tiled oval hood is suspended from the ceiling over an oval island. Adding drama above the cooking surface, early colonial stove hoods were plastered and very simple in design. Today, these concrete structures sometimes soar eighteen feet to meet old beamed ceilings, grandly accentuating a room's height. Often boldly painted to contrast with the wall color, stove hoods may be decorated along their bottom edges with bas-relief patterns or glazed accent tiles. Vertical fluting has also been a popular design detail, as seen in many colonial kitchens including Hacienda La Casa Grande de Apaseo in Guanajuato.

Inside Mexican kitchens, white and golden yellows—with brick-red or rich blues as accents—are the predominant colors we have encountered in our design work and hacienda research. In response to high interest from homeowners and designers in adapting Mexico's traditional paint colors, we have replicated the old-world hacienda hues in our Hacienda Style Color Palette with Pittsburgh® Paints in order to celebrate and spread Mexico's rich color legacy. In addition to brightening walls, doors and stove hoods, color also graces kitchen floors, thanks to Mexican concrete floor tiles that are beautiful in a variety of solid or patterned hues, including goldenrod and terra-cotta. Their cool surfaces are easy to maintain and the design possibilities limitless. Striking designs can be achieved from grouping patterned tiles together in a central square or diamond, surrounded by a polished concrete border that frames the patterned tiles.

Painted or stenciled designs annunciate doorways, counterfronts or walls and bring special decorative interest. The kitchen at Los Dos features elegantly-patterned stencils around windows, doorways and along the top of the wainscot. As the owners wanted to soften the feel of the heavy, high walls, they adapted a handmade detail from their Talavera tile and had it replicated into a stencil design around these areas. For their regal, brick-red stove hood, a medallion design from an old Victorian stencil book provided the perfect decorative edging to the solid red. Colonial style design elements continue to enjoy unsurpassed attention in both restoration and new contemporary construction projects.

PAGE 102: *The Talavera tile backsplash at Casa Shubin extends vertically to accent the room's extreme height.*

PAGE 103: *This restored colonial hacienda kitchen features a dramatic stove hood accented with handpainted ceramic tile in the Yucatán.*

OPPOSITE: *At Hacienda El Alto in Morelia, colonial stencil patterns elegantly anchor a wooden countertop and offer contrast to the stainless steel stove hood.*

LEFT: An elegant, grand space, the restored kitchen at Hacienda Chenche de las Torres in the Yucatán features lofty ceilings, high windows, a bold stove hood and artfully tiled backsplash.

OPPOSITE: The deep blue and rust ceramic tiles of this restored Mérida kitchen complements the patterned, antique, concrete floor tiles. Design by Fritz Menzel and Werner Gross, Yucatán.

PAGE 108: A functional, tiled island features an inset marble top and traditional blue and white Talavera tiles. Casa Staub-Meyers.

PAGE 109: In Mérida, Casa Santana's old colonial charm emanates from its original elements including painted doors, patterned floor tiles, sculptural stove hood and alacena, (wall cabinet).

Many of these old tiles—removed from their colonial surfaces during restoration projects—have become popular elements to introduce into new kitchens. Because of limited availability, they are best used in smaller focus areas such as a nicho, or as counter or backsplash accents. A variety of color and glaze across a tiled surface is commonplace in old Mexican kitchens, and has been through the centuries.

Restored Haciendas

INTRICATELY LINKED TO THE LAND AND THEIR WORKING PAST, MEXICAN

HACIENDAS—EVEN THOSE IN THE MOST CRUMBLING STATE OF DISREPAIR—

CAN ENJOY A SECOND LIFE WITH AN EYE TOWARDS SENSITIVE RESTORATION.

Original elements discovered intact are highlighted, sometimes moved to a new

location within the property, or adapted for a new function. When only partially

intact, the original design of an element can be salvaged to serve as a template to

replicate a new, functioning version of the source. Unique corbel designs, old

spindled window grilles, painted stencil patterns, wrought-iron light fixtures and

tile patterns have been revived, relocated and re-used in these ways.

The revelations of a hacienda's past appear in innovative ways. Portions of

old stone walls can be left exposed to show original rubblestone construction and

juxtapose with newly stuccoed wall areas. Or original stencils might be newly

framed as decorative art, while old patterned concrete floor tiles are salvaged

and replaced in wall nichos or on kitchen islands. Old wellheads are retooled to

become fountains, and stone feeding troughs become unique sinks.

◆◆◆◆◆◆◆◆◆◆◆

OPPOSITE AND ABOVE:
*Elegant stencils, wood door
frames and antiques decorate
the* comedor *of Hacienda
Itzincab, Yucatán.*

Particularly striking as decorative art are industrial relics from the Yucatán's era of henequén processing. Iron machinery parts and wheels, wooden machine molds, iron rail tracks, water tanks and aqueducts have all found new expressions. Machine wheels are integrated into walls as window elements or strung up on steel wires to create artistic sculptural displays. Rail tracks are embedded into courtyard walls as sun sculpture and feeding troughs become lily ponds and fountain bases, while wooden machine molds are newly fashioned into mirror frames. Corbels, once ceiling-high beam supports, come down the wall to eye level to display favored santos and art objects as seen at Hacienda Chenché de las Torres.

The enchantments of hacienda restoration are many. Unusual discoveries can show themselves amidst the estate's grounds, in storerooms or even underground. Restoration clean-up at a roofless Hacienda Xixim turned up an old shell-shaped carved stone, which became a showcase piece in a wall nicho at the entrance to the casa principal. An unusual discovery that started "underground" but over the years rose quickly above ground is evidenced at Hacienda San José Cholul. In the bathroom of guest room number nine stands a massive ceiba tree, encircled by a ceiling aperture that allows its canopy-free reign. Through years of abandonment at Hacienda San José Cholul, roofless rooms gave way to jungle growth and the surging of the tree that is considered sacred by the Maya. Given floor lighting to "honor" it, the tree is a commanding and awe-inspiring guest in the suite.

At Hacienda Santa Cruz, large iron wheels displayed against the *casa de máquina*'s rich earthy orange facade signal the wheels' working past. On the building's west side, the tall chimney and original water tank work together as an inviting restful retreat, as owner Fiona St. Clair uncovered the tank's myriad water channels that served in the distribution of water. After sifting through mounds of the original collapsed roof, workers cleaning up the estate's private chapel turned up its original hardwood ceiling corbels, miraculously preserved despite decades of exposure. Today, the golden yellow concrete floor and walls of the chapel are aglow thanks to St. Clair's addition of a trio of skylights above the altar.

A unique showcase of Yucatán's magnificent henequén era, Hacienda Sotuta de Peón has been brought back to life as a working hacienda, allowing visitors to step back in time to experience the grandeur of hacienda life. Today, the vast estate produces and processes henequén using machinery and technology from the late nineteenth century in an impressive setting surrounded by dramatic henequén fields. Beautifully restored by the Shangri-La Group, the estate's casa principal features elegant antique-filled rooms that open to grand arcaded portales overlooking the estate's extensive gardens, pool and restaurant.

TOP: *The arcaded facade of Hacienda Yodzonot's elegant guesthouse is rich with color and architectural ornament.*

ABOVE: *A young foal, Muy Bien, is the newest member of the hacienda's stable of horses.*

OPPOSITE: *The back portal at Hacienda Yodzonot displays an old carved-wood element against a warm colorful wall.*

Hacienda Yodzonot

Hidden between tranquil Mayan villages amidst lush Yucatán vegetation, Hacienda Yodzonot is a true jewel in the jungle. Owners Christopher Holder and Margaret Andrews have restored the elegant old estate with great attention to detail, inspired by the region's natural materials, local artisans and centuries-old paint and stone-carving traditions.

Myriad corrals and jumping rings for the couple's magnificent horses are surrounded by the warm earthen orange color gracing Yodzonot's arcaded buildings: the casa principal, newly-constructed guesthouse and horse stables. Selecting the estate's lime-based paint color, created with natural pigments and the experienced hand of a local craftsman, was high on the couple's priority list, as the main house had been previously painted an unattractive green by a former owner.

Inside and out, the decor of Yodzonot is a testament to Holder and Andrews's unique design style and their passion for the region's history and traditions. Treasured remnants from the estate include pre-Hispanic carved stone vessels, one of which has become a charmingly simple bathroom sink. The exterior wall of the newly expanded kitchen has benefited from the addition of an old stone *pila* (trough), found on the grounds and now partially embedded in the wall. Captivating shapes of other larger, local stones—offered to the couple from the back of a pickup—were integrated into the kitchen doorway surround, their sculptural forms boldly beckoning entry.

As the alluring textures of local limestone also testify, the theme of stone is prominent throughout Yodzonot. The special carved-stone surrounds for doors and windows that Andrews designed create a textural contrast to the colorful painted walls. Brought to life by an expert Maya artisan, the myriad surrounds and their relief designs prompt thoughtful appreciation of the skill required to intricately carve floral, bird and other ornate motifs. This deeply rooted stone-carving tradition from the region's ancient Maya civilization is practiced daily in the surrounding villages.

Other custom details at Yodzonot include wrought-iron grilles that dress up both building windows as well as horse stable doors, some beautifully incorporating horseshoe motifs in their decorative top crests. A statuesque reflection of the equestrian environs, carved wooden folk art horses from Guatemala posture on the front porch amidst guest chairs.

OPPOSITE AND ABOVE: *Carved-stone door surrounds and decorative wrought-iron grilles offer textural contrast to the colorful painted walls. Hacienda Yodzonot, Yucatán.*

ABOVE: *In the Yucatán,
elegant carved-stone columns
create an impressive entrance
to Hacienda Xcumpich, Mérida.*

OPPOSITE: *Colorful walls
offer a rich backdrop for owner
Silviane Boucher's collection of
antiques and contemporary
paintings. Hacienda Xcumpich,
Mérida, Yucatán.*

Hacienda Xcumpich

Secluded behind old stone walls, Hacienda Xcumpich reveals stately, elegant arches that frame the casa principal's front portico. Faithfully restored to its original splendor by owner/archaeologist Silviane Boucher, Xcumpich is a haven of practicality and comfort, no less a showcase for the owner's intriguing assemblage of paintings, photos and sculptures. Collected from famous Mexican artists and her local artist friends, Boucher's array of artworks are lovingly placed throughout the estate amidst a palette of colorful walls and tiled floors. Striking juxtapositions abound in her mix of Moroccan and Mexican pieces, antiques and unique objects, such as the hanging, henequén light fixture by Rafael Garcia and carved wooden angel wing sculpture posturing above an old antique clock, for example. Boucher's inspiration for the various tones of yellow that grace most of the hacienda's interior was prompted by the simple allure of the mango and earthy-reddish exterior that serves as a warm and natural complement to the yellows.

The principal adaptations Boucher made to the property included the conversion of some of the hacienda's original doorways to tall windows. With more than fifteen doors inside the estate, not all were necessary as passageways, and by simply filling in the bottom areas of the openings, windows were created. A door situated in a hallway made the conversion to a window with the bonus of a newly-designed window seat that gives views to the garden. To increase livable space, Boucher enclosed the back portal with floor-to-ceiling windows to create a room that fully welcomes the garden.

OPPOSITE: Originally the open-air portal, the space was enclosed with large windows, providing lush garden views, Hacienda Xcumpich.

THIS PAGE: Natural light spills into Hacienda Xcumpich's colorful dining room thanks to tall windows converted from the hacienda's original doorways.

ABOVE: *A lush landscape surrounds the impressive facade of* Hacienda Chenché de las Torres, *Yucatán.*

OPPOSITE: *The casa principal's grand sala features original floor tile, antique furnishings and painted wall designs re-created from the originals.* Hacienda Chenché de las Torres, *Yucatán.*

Hacienda Chenché de las Torres

Presently located east of Mérida and dating from the eighteenth century, Hacienda Chenché de las Torres resembles a medieval European fortress with crenellated towers and grand-scale architectural features. One of the Yucatán's most prosperous haciendas during the henequén boom years, Chenché featured interiors with considerable ornamentation, much of which needed extensive restoration following years of abandonment.

Owner Isabelle Kimmelman first fell in love with Chenché de las Torres through photos she viewed while at home in Europe. Her dream had been to find an old castle or fortress that offered both a mild climate and the opportunity for beautiful gardens. After reading about Mérida, she planned a trip to view properties in Yucatán, Quintana Roo and Belize, but only made it to the Yucatán. It was love at first sight when she visited Chenché de las Torres. Immediately smitten with the high ceilings, tall columns, stucco ornamentation (which includes the original family's coat of arms), painted wall designs and extensive gardens, Kimmelman became committed to preserving the historical elements and began plans for a faithful restoration.

Four years later, the restoration work was complete and Chenché de las Torres was a revived jewel. The adventure of bringing the hacienda back to life enabled Kimmelman to draw on the inspiring talent of local workers, as well as her own creativity with the kitchen redesign and tiling. She especially enjoyed adapting found elements to new uses. She rescued old beams and had them cut into three-inch-thick planks to form the massive dining table. An old balustrade found in one of the estate's storehouses was used to fashion legs for the massive table, and the remainder of the old beam wood was used for the dining chairs.

Original stencil and floor tile designs at Chenché de las Torres were revived with the help of existing patterns. Inside the entire casa principal, with the exception of the kitchen, were ornate wall stencils. Where they were damaged or missing, mylar templates were used to copy and re-create the stencils. Similarly, many of the casa's rooms, excepting the dining and living room, had areas of badly broken concrete floor tiles. Kimmelman selected old-style patterns that complimented the room's wall colors and stencils and had these concrete tiles made by a local factory.

Today, Kimmelman has seen her hacienda home dream come true. The estate's pool, resting in the shadow of one of the hacienda's tall crenellated towers and surrounded by lush, flowering plants, is one of her favorite indulgences. She savors the ancient atmosphere and enjoys imagining what Chenché de las Torres might have been like in its heyday.

OPPOSITE: At Hacienda Chenché de las Torres, old stencil designs were revived throughout, including the estate's dramatic dining room. The three-inch-thick tabletop was fashioned from old found ceiling beams rescued by owner Isabelle Kimmelman.

ABOVE AND RIGHT: The back portal of the hacienda is a relaxed, elegant space featuring unique stencils and wooden corbels as decorative wall accents. Yucatán.

Hacienda El Alto

OPPOSITE: *Hacienda El Alto's central courtyard is resplendent with stately, colonial stone arches and contemporary stone spheres. Morelia, Michoacán.*

PAGE 128: *The arcaded portal at Hacienda El Alto features an elegant blend of antiques, contemporary art and colonial furnishings and accents. Morelia, Michoacán.*

PAGE 129: *A colonial painted armario (armoire) houses a fine collection of religious relics, Hacienda El Alto. Morelia, Michoacán.*

Located in Michoacán, Hacienda El Alto dates from approximately 1600 and was one of the first five buildings in Morelia, the capital city. Restored to its original colonial splendor by Ed Holler and Sam Saunders, the hacienda is so named for its elevated siting near the region's main aqueduct. The extensive agricultural estate consisted primarily of orchards, cattle and horses. As the city grew, Hacienda El Alto also became an important distribution center for produce from outlying farms and haciendas.

Today, the 12,000-square-foot hacienda compound includes the casa principal, resplendent with stately stone arches, columns and ornate carved stone details. The high-ceilinged rooms of the house look onto the central courtyard, two sides of which feature covered portales that are elegantly furnished with colonial antiques, art and ceramics. Avid collectors and antique dealers, Holler and Saunders have maximized an inviting, sumptuous atmosphere at El Alto with their special collection of colonial furniture from Mexico, South America and Asia, giving a solid base to offset their religious relics, contemporary paintings and large-scale pottery and exotic mineral specimens.

In the center of the courtyard, a colonial stone wellhead retooled as a simple fountain now holds court with multiple massive stone spheres. Made of two halves of fused, crushed stone, the hollowed spheres were designed by the owners and bring a contemporary sculptural touch to the ancient space. Original cattle corrals were reconfigured and higher stone walls constructed to create a second private courtyard and reflecting pool. From the pool area, a newly created stone stairwell leads to rooftop living quarters, built atop the adjacent original building now used for entertaining.

An unusual discovery made during the restoration process was that of an underground tunnel in the main courtyard. Additional investigation revealed that the tunnel led to a nearby monastery, indicating its probable history as a clandestine travel route in earlier epochs.

ABOVE AND OPPOSITE:
*Color enlivens the castellated
facade of Casa Nueva.
Restoration and design by
architect Salvador Reyes Ríos
and designer Josefina Larraín.
Casa de Máquina de Hacienda
Sacchich. Yucatán.*

Casa de Máquina de Hacienda Sacchich

Tucked away in a small Mayan village not far from the pre-Hispanic ruins of Acanceh, the 150-year-old *Casa de Máquina* of Hacienda Sacchich is announced by a towering 80-foot chimney. The lush jungle drive leading to the compound opens to reveal the corner turrets and castellated roof lines of the massive, fortress-like stone buildings. Current owners Howie and Cyndy Berger and daughter Brianna were intrigued by the "regal, solid feeling" of the buildings, whose 22-foot ceilings and 3-foot-thick walls were surrounded by beautiful gardens. Already partially renovated, the Bergers aimed to continue Sacchich's restoration by incorporating contemporary architectural design and staying true to the structure's rich history and building techniques. Working together with architect Salvador Reyes Ríos and designer Josefina Larraín, the family has seen their dreams realized.

Following years of abandonment, the Casa de Máquina was rescued in the early '90s from ruin by owners Josefina Larraín and Paul Fullerton. Adeptly tackling the extensive cleanup and restoration, Fullerton and Larraín transformed the machine house into a residence and re-roofed the packing house for use as Fullerton's sculpture studio. Visiting Hacienda Sacchich in 1998, we were impressed by its initial reincarnation, documented in our second book, *The New Hacienda*. When we learned of its continued unfolding, we were excited to return almost eight years later to photograph the results.

The Casa de Máquina compound—three limestone buildings in a U-shape with a central courtyard—has a storied past and an equally rich restoration history. Dating from the turn of the nineteenth to twentieth century, henequén fiber was processed here as it was on many Yucatán haciendas dating from that time.

The west building, donned *Casa Vieja* by the Bergers, linked to the chimney and water tank-turned-swimming pool, and housed the iron wheels and beams once part of the steam-driven engine system. In the east building—*Casa Nueva*—henequén fibers were compressed and stored in bales. Between these two on the south side is the *Tren de Raspa*, a raised open-air building home to the fiber-extracting machine. Rail cars would pass below the platform to collect fresh henequén fibers en route to nearby drying fields.

Phase One of reconstruction focused on converting the packing house or Casa Nueva into three bedrooms and bathrooms. Previously Fullerton's studio, the space still retained much of its original look and patina, with the exception of the roof restoration and addition of a large skylight.

In order to create three separate bathrooms and baths within the 2000-square-foot rectangular building, one side became a 1000-square-foot master suite and the other side was divided to create two separate bedrooms with private baths. A dramatic central hallway is the entrance to all three rooms. With soaring 26-foot ceilings, and 13-foot-high doors and windows, the owners maintained the airy, open feeling of the master suite, flowing the bedroom, living area and bathroom into this grand 54-foot-long space.

ABOVE AND OPPOSITE:
*Custom furnishings, curtains
and countertops were scaled to
match the dramatic height and
grandeur of Casa Nueva's
master suite. Renovation
and design by Salvador Reyes
Ríos and Josefina Larraín.*

The north end of the master suite became a sunken living area, which took advantage of a hole left in the floor that had been dynamited to create a large casting pit for sculptures. The Bergers wanted to keep the original feature, but didn't know what it should be. Reyes Ríos created the *sala baja*, the sunken living area. The south end of the building became the bathroom suite which opens onto a newly created outdoor plunge pool and patio.

Reyes Ríos's signature design concept is to identify and integrate the spirit of the original building in new design. The height and grandeur in the bedrooms was captured in his custom furnishings scaled to match the proportions of the room. The cedar bed and two 9-foot-tall armoires feature iron grillwork inspired by the room's original architectural details and doors. To ensure privacy between the suite's spaces, but retain the overall perception of spaciousness, Reyes Ríos created large white ceiling curtains and floor-to-ceiling wood screens crafted from stainless steel and Brazilian hardwood slats. The screens, fondly referred to by the Bergers as marimbas, promote the illusion of soft translucent walls while the white ceiling curtains responding to incoming breezes create the sense of fluidity the new design sought.

Inside the Casa Nueva, Reyes Ríos created an innovative design detail that acts to reduce the wall's extreme height to a more human scale. A 14-inch "band" of the original wall, left unpainted, uniquely exhibits the streaked and time-worn gray textures born of years of ceiling leakage. Wrapping around the entire perimeter of the room, the stripe focuses the eye and unifies the suites' spaces in sensitive respect for the wall's weathered past.

In the guest bedrooms of Casa Nueva, the color palettes of painted wall stripes and solid geometric floor tiles create an inviting, artful atmosphere. Again utilizing the concept of a horizontal wall band—this time in repetition—Larraín innovatively painted the walls to mimic the common hacienda visual of vigas, large ceiling beams. By allowing the graphic of the beams to travel down the walls, a visual counterbalance is achieved that offsets the rooms' extreme height.

ABOVE: *The master suite's private patio and plunge pool are surrounded by a unique fence of hand-stacked rocks in open steel cages.*

OPPOSITE AND TOP:
Once the estate's former water tank, the reinvented, tranquil pool features stone buttresses and a shady bamboo and steel pergola. Restoration and design by architect Salvador Reyes Ríos. Casa de Máquina de Hacienda Sacchich.

In the adjoining guest bathrooms, the stripes continue to play up the rooms' height. As a solution to the rooms' narrow width, Reyes Ríos designed a tall, narrow mirror to echo the space above the sink counter, creating a new perception of scale without changing the rooms' proportions. A newly created frosted glass wall/door in this bathroom allows diffused light to enter, yet gives privacy.

The Bergers' approach to landscaping at Hacienda Sacchich was paved by Josefina Larraín's horticultural expertise. As the prior owner of the compound, she had planted every tree and plant on the property, orchestrating the landscape's lush revival.

At the south end of Casa Vieja, the original water tank was reinvented as a swimming pool. The pool's slightly raised walls and solid buttresses lend structural support and pose as sculptural accents against the green blanket of grass. At one end, a new steel and bamboo pergola creates a relaxing refuge from the tropical sun.

Framing the expansive gardens, *albarradas* (low walls of dry-stacked stone traditionally used to mark property lines) are given a contemporary twist: local limestone rocks are newly encased in open steel cages. Integrating well with the landscape, the rocks were hand stacked and placed within the cages.

Phase Two renovation of Hacienda Sacchich will target the *Tren de Raspa*, or Loggia, as it is now called. The platform will be dropped to ground level, opening up the central courtyard. Water features are planned off the columns of the loggia in the central courtyard and the back side, and a circular staircase, designed to mimic the nearby original water tower, will lead visitors to a rooftop stargazing and living area.

Soon after, Phase Three will update the Casa Vieja, which currently has three bedrooms, a living room, one bathroom and the kitchen. While the existing living room and kitchen layout will remain, a loft bedroom, not original to the house, will be eliminated to leave two bedrooms. The central bathroom will be moved to an existing bedroom and replaced with a central hallway that will allow a straight visual from the entryway to the swimming pool.

A sunken living area anchors the north end of the spacious master suite. This unique "sala baja" took advantage of a hole left in the floor that had been dynamited to create a large casting pit for sculptures. Design by architect Salvador Reyes Ríos, Casa de Máquina de Hacienda Sacchich.

Despite the labors of restoring Hacienda Sacchich, the Bergers have never looked back, and are amazed at the ease and speed with which restorations have progressed, and the beautiful results achieved through the collaboration with Salvador Reyes Ríos and Josefina Larraín. Living at Hacienda Sacchich has increased their respect for the economic and social interdependence between a hacienda and its village in days gone by. Even more, their hacienda living experience has, literally, restored their senses.

"The hacienda is usually an extension of the village beyond and they are historically bound together. When at a hacienda you cannot help but understand that. So, when spending time at Sacchich, everything from the sounds of the children playing on the playground, to the barking dogs, to the strangely beautiful caterpillar that silently glides by, all mingle together to create the experience. Being at our hacienda is like sensory rehabilitation for us. It sharpens all of our senses."

OPPOSITE: At the Casa de Máquina de Hacienda Sacchich, a tall narrow mirror and wall stripes play up this bathroom's height. A frosted glass door allows diffused light yet gives privacy.

THIS PAGE: Painted wall stripes and solid geometric floor tiles create a colorful palette in this guest bedroom. Design by Josefina Larraín.

Colonial Style

THE COLONIAL PERIOD FROM POSTCONQUEST TO 1821—THE YEAR OF MEXICO'S INDEPENDENCE FROM SPAIN—BROUGHT A VARIETY OF ARCHITECTURAL DESIGN INFLUENCES TO THE STATELY CITY HOMES AND RURAL HACIENDAS BEING BUILT DURING THIS TIME. In contrast to the more austere, fortress-like designs of early sixteenth-century buildings, the ethos of Mexico's colonial-era design was one of decorative ornamentation, and was predominately influenced by baroque, Gothic, Moorish, neoclassical, Victorian and Renaissance designs.

Although different in form and function, town houses and working country estates shared common design denominators throughout the colonial period. Architectural features, including ceiling beams, columns, doors, window grilles, floor tiles, lime-based paint and wall stencils, were used in both haciendas and colonial homes. The colonial architectural style and its decorative elements continued to be used in new construction following independence—especially in the southern regions of Yucatán, Campeche and Chiapas that are a great distance from central Mexico—therefore it is common for these later, "colonial-style" buildings (built in the mid to late 1800s) to possess colonial-era attributes.

◆◆◆◆◆◆◆◆◆◆◆

OPPOSITE: *Suliram, restored by artist/designer Raymond Branham, features grand-scale spaces alive with rich color, pattern and artful design accents.*

ABOVE: *An ornate iron grill frames a view to the light-filled atrium, Suliram, Mérida, Yucatán.*

During the distinct period of heightened economic prosperity spurred during the reign of Mexico president Porfirio Díaz (1876–1911), buildings reflected this new appetite for luxury which made architectural opulence the vogue, especially French-influenced embellishments. In addition to new buildings sporting neoclassical arches, columns and elaborate friezes, older buildings were often given a face-lift, as exteriors were updated with highly decorative pediments (*frontones*) over doors and windows, ironwork and lavish stucco ornamentation.

OPPOSITE: *Vibrant color, ornate ironwork and restored stucco ornamentation add decorative interest to Mérida's Casa Reyes-Larraín.*

THIS PAGE: *Frontones, or decorative pediments, top iron grilled windows in a variety of designs. Mérida, Yucatán.*

ABOVE: A *tranquil pond harbors exotic water plants and an old stone trough.*

OPPOSITE: *Merimo Nah's verdant courtyard features a unique water garden that runs the length of the raised swimming pool. Restoration and design by architect Salvador Reyes Ríos and designer Josefina Larraín. Mérida, Yucatán.*

PAGES 146–147: *Merimo Nah's* záguan *offers views to the arcaded portal and lush gardens. A bamboo mirror, custom bench and ceramic pot posture against green walls.*

Merimo Nah

Secluded behind an elegant neoclassical facade in Mérida's historic district, Merimo Nah draws its name from a combination of Mérida and Montreal—the owner's two residences—and *nah*, the Maya word for home. Luxuriating in soothing outdoor water spaces and gracious architectural features, the home dates from the late nineteenth century.

Sometime after its first renovation, the colonial-style home was transformed into a factory that produced a traditional rice-coconut beverage. This utilitarian phase of the structure's existence resulted in the removal and storage of many of the home's original elements: doors, window pediments and beautiful patterned concrete tiles. Contrary to common practice at the time, these elements were not sold or recycled but carefully stored in the home. Their presence inspired architect Salvador Reyes Ríos and designer Josefina Larraín to collaborate closely with the owners on a home restoration and expansion plan that would utilize and preserve as much of the original details as possible. The result is a living space that completely embraces the owners' love of nature, water and open-air living in a streamlined design.

Stepping from the street into the záguan of Merimo Nah, one is enveloped by soothing green walls enclosing the heart of the house that is both water haven and sculpture. Visible from almost every interior room, a verdant courtyard alive with bougainvillea, heliconia and queen palms and is sided by open portales stretching down the east and west sides of the rectangle. Adjacent to the arcaded west portal, a tranquil pond anchored by a centuries-old stone pila harbors exotic aquatic plants. A few steps away, an elongated, rectangular water garden home to palms and papyrus runs the length of the courtyard wall, serving as a protective border between the rich orange-red kancab wall and the raised swimming pool.

Merimo Nah's courtyard was created by constructing a new building on the east side that joined with the original L-shaped house and neighboring wall. The home's water tank, once used to collect rainwater from the roof, was adeptly enlarged and transformed by Reyes Ríos into a circular staircase that serves as an anchor between the old and new buildings, and the ascent to a rooftop terrace.

Enlivened with rich color and a wealth of old, decorative floor tiles, Merimo Nah's elegant interiors pay homage to the home's strong architectural details and showcase the owner's unique global finds. The carefully choreographed mix of antiques, artwork and custom furniture in wood, stone, iron and fiber celebrates timeless materials in inventive ways.

In the colorful *sala*, a painting by a Mérida artist neighbors a rare body armor of bone platelets from the Indonesian island of Sulawesi. Stone-topped tables hold traditional Talavera ceramics, newly adapted to lamps with zigzag-patterned shades that echo the ceramic design. Underfoot, antique patterned concrete tiles original to the house are framed with newly made solid tiles and a polished white cement border, creating a trio of textural interest. The room's nineteen-foot-high ceiling beams—painted blue—increase geometric interest and the parameters of innovative design.

The textures of the pomegranate-hued walls in the formal *comedor* (dining room) come alive throughout the day with a changing palette of light delivered through the ceiling skylights on either end of the room. Woven chairs and a custom cedar table by Reyes Ríos rest on a visual carpet of antique patterned cement tiles.

Stone is a reigning presence at Merimo Nah. Thanks to the creativity of Reyes Ríos and Larraín, its luxuriant textures are the artful focus of both living spaces and the outdoor courtyard and gardens. In the courtyard, rough-cut stone pavers blend beautifully with walkways of washed concrete that blend white cement, sand and local *sascab* (white earth). Freestanding garden walls hold thousands of hand-chinked stones, a salute to the region's traditional rajueleado technique that features chinked stone surfaces. Under the open-air portal, a carved-stone base with unique geometric angles artfully supports a dining table.

OPPOSITE AND ABOVE:
The colorful spacious sala at Merimo Nah features old patterned concrete tiles. Among the artful treasures are a painting by a Mérida artist and a rare body armor made of bone platelets from Sulawesi, Indonesia.

ABOVE: *Merimo Nah's kitchen door opens onto the lush central courtyard.*

OPPOSITE: *Against the backdrop of warm yellow walls, Merimo Nah's cocina blends glazed Talavera-style tile with colorful concrete floor tiles. A polished concrete island offers storage and work space. Design by architect Salvador Reyes Ríos and designer Josefina Larraín.*

Inside the sala, carved limestone forms serve as console and side tables. In the bathrooms, custom stone vessel sinks posture atop counters—their roughly chiseled exteriors rounded out with smooth, polished interiors. Inspired by the wooden corbels commonly seen supporting beams in Yucatán haciendas and homes, Reyes Ríos designed custom wooden spouts as faucets. Andiroba, a Brazilian tropical wood, was used for the sink counters to add contrast to the white limestone.

Merimo Nah's newly designed kitchen centers around a cook-friendly, polished concrete island creating both storage and work space, inset with a cutting board for convenience. Anchoring the room is a sculptural stove hood, a traditional feature of many old Yucatán kitchens. The original kitchen (now a guest room) had a smaller, similar style hood which served as inspiration for the newly constructed feature. Against the backdrop of warm yellow walls, the kitchen brings together traditional glazed Talavera-style tiles and solid white, yellow and gray cement floor tiles in a bold geometric statement. Adding visual warmth to the breadth of tile, cedarwood cabinets consolidate necessary storage and serve to visually connect the stove and refrigerator.

LEFT: The light-filled master bathroom features a hardwood counter and custom stone sink designed by Salvador Reyes Ríos. A tall, thin mirror and onyx sconce accentuate the room's lofty ceilings.

OPPOSITE: Tall shuttered windows bring natural light and fresh breezes to the guest bedroom. Two custom beds are draped in soft white netting.

FOLLOWING PAGE: Pomegranate-hued walls are a dramatic backdrop for a Mexican colonial painting in Merimo Nah's dining room. Designed by Salvador Reyes Ríos, a dining table rests upon original, patterned concrete tiles. Bamboo brush-column light fixtures were designed by Josefina Larraín and crafted by Yucatán Bamboo.

PAGE 155: A custom daybed draped in colorful stripes is a bold contrast to the original, patterned floor tiles at Merimo Nah, Mérida, Yucatán.

LEFT: *Merimo Nah's rooftop terrace features comfortable, cushioned daybeds, ideal for siestas and starlit evenings.*

BOTTOM: *Running the length of the courtyard, a custom-designed awning provides shade and protection from the rain. Garden design by Josefina Larraín.*

ABOVE: *An antique* santo
keeps a watchful eye over
Merimo Nah's comfortable
open-air portal.

ABOVE: *Rich architectural ornament and saturated color enliven the facade of* La Casa del Pocito, *Mérida, Yucatán.*

OPPOSITE: *Terra-cotta–hued stone walls create a warm and inviting backdrop for a Mayan cross and a collection of antique stoneware artfully displayed in an aqueous blue-green nicho,* La Casa del Pocito. *Design by Jim Neeley and David Dow.*

La Casa del Pocito

Tucked away on a quiet downtown Mérida street, La Casa del Pocito is an artful haven of robust color and pared-down luxury, setting the stage for a stellar assemblage of artwork, antiques and found relics—many of them newly reinvented in the hands of designers/owners Jim Neeley and David Dow. Composed of equal parts personal design intention, the ingenuity of local craftsmen and multicultural serendipity, La Casa del Pocito echoes the relaxed gracious interiors Neeley and Dow experienced in their global travels and frequent visits to Andalucia in southern Spain, Morocco and Italy.

Restored years earlier by renowned architect Salvador Reyes Ríos, the colonial-style home was updated with modern systems while maintaining its original character—eighteen-foot ceilings, patterned concrete floor tiles and thick stone walls. The owners focused on comfortable furnishings that worked within the scale of the rooms, and created minimal compositions combining old-world lighting that best offset their unique collection of art and antiques. A strong indoor-outdoor relationship allows the modest, two-bedroom townhouse to extend its reach. Most of the rooms of "Pocito" spill either into the intimate, fountained central courtyard or the rear walled garden anchored by a Moorish-inspired pool.

Based in Sonoma County in Northern California where they have another home, Neeley and Dow enthusiastically embraced the rich palette of the Yucatán, a welcome contrast to the neutral, noncolor palette favored in California design. By reconditioning the walls with traditional lime paint hues from the Yucatán, they conjured the richness of curry, clay and *marmadol*—a local, luscious yellow papaya. In the terra-cotta–hued dining room, a nicho was repainted a delicate, aqueous blue-green, a perfect pairing to showcase the owners' collection of white stoneware pieces, prized for their somewhat chipped, less than perfect condition. Cool celadon dresses the master bedroom and a vibrant blue holds court in the kitchen, providing balance to bright yellow ceramic tile.

ABOVE, RIGHT AND
OPPOSITE: *Vibrant yellow
ocher walls, old French roof
tiles and a tranquil fountain
add character to the intimate
courtyard at La Casa del
Pocito, Mérida, Yucatán.*

PAGE 162: *Antique patterned
concrete tile creates a dramatic
wainscot in the guest bathroom.*

PAGE 163: *Designed by Jim
Neeley, this four-poster bed is
crowned by eighteenth-century
altar elements. Echoing the
linear profile of the bed spires
are lamps crafted from antique
Italian altar candlesticks.*

Designed by Neeley and beautifully crafted by a local carpenter, eighteenth-century altar elements found in Mérida became crowning flourishes atop the guest bedroom's four-poster bed. Echoing the tall linear profile of the bed spires are bedside lamps crafted from similarly

dated Italian altar candlesticks discovered by the owners while traveling in Argentina.

With views to the newly built pool, the master bedroom features a locally made, wrought-iron canopy bed. In the master bath, multiple gold frames were fitted with mirrors to create a wall montage above the tiled counter.

For the dining room chandelier, Neeley wanted a large-scale piece to fill the volume of the high dining room without resorting to the heavy mass of wrought iron. Inspired by an Italian style chandelier, he adapted turned wood tassels, once table legs, to the piece's arms and completed the task with custom paint and gilding. The resulting chandelier seems to float over the dining table and offers a delicate transparency that doesn't outweigh the room.

Throughout the refurbishing of La Casa del Pocito, Neeley and Dow found the experience, sensibility and ingenuity of their local Mayan workers inspiring.

To update the guest bath, Neeley added large antique concrete tiles as a wainscot. In response to the unfinished raw edge of tile, a worker cut a 3/4 by 12-inch pvc pipe in half lengthwise and filled it with white cement—creating the perfectly-shaped and textured radius detail to join wall and richly colored patterned tile.

Uncovered by Neeley and Dow in Spain, a collection of 60-year-old Spanish lottery cards hang in multiples upon the studio wall, creating a colorful, graphic accent to the rich orange walls. The black iron floor lamp, created by melding a custom iron base to an antique Spanish lantern, contrasts beautifully with the room's chairs and sofa upholstered in pure Belgian linen. In the sala and studio, sisal rugs add contrast and warmth to cool tile floors newly framed with polished concrete borders.

OPPOSITE: *A collection of old Spanish lottery cards creates a colorful graphic statement on the studio walls at La Casa del Pocito. Design by Jim Neeley and David Dow.*

THIS PAGE: *La Casa del Pocito's richly painted sala blends distinguished portraits, tin Spanish Colonial Revival sconces, a rustic Mayan table and comfortable seating.*

OPPOSITE AND RIGHT:
*An old stone capital was
creatively adapted to become a
fountain accent for the newly
designed swimming pool.
La Casa del Pocito, Mérida.*

PAGE 168: *An old iron
window grille was beautifully
adapted as a decorative base
for a narrow hallway table at
La Casa del Pocito, Mérida.*

In order to adapt an old stone capital as a fountain accent for the newly designed pool, workers bored a center hole vertically, and then sculpted a channel atop the capital for water flow. The challenge of creating the perfect trickle and water path was met by cutting a groove in the stone's bottom to create an even cascade of water across the face of stone and into the inviting pool.

OPPOSITE: *With lush views to the pool and walled garden, the master bedroom features a custom, wrought-iron bed. La Casa del Pocito, Mérida.*

An old iron window grille discovered by Neeley at a local antique dealer struck him as the perfect size for adapting as a base for a narrow entry hall table. Upon closer inspection, he realized it was the same iron design fronting the neighboring two town homes, built coincident with La Casa del Pocito. Though not hailing from Spain or another far-flung locale, the piece was especially welcome inside the home. Sometimes the best discoveries are found right around the corner.

ABOVE: *The restored facade of Casa de los Artistas, Izamal.*

OPPOSITE: *The central courtyard of Casa de los Artistas is a mesmerizing mix of color and texture. Architect Salvador Reyes Ríos created a sculptural "sun clock" from hacienda iron rail tracks.*

FOLLOWING PAGE: *Architect Salvador Reyes Ríos and designer Josefina Larraín combined inviting color and concrete tiles for an elegantly simple dining room.*

PAGE 173: *Casa de los Artistas is an artful study in textures: handchiseled stone pavers, smooth yellow concrete tile and an iron table topped with glazed tiles.*

Casa de los Artistas

Located east of Mérida, Izamal is one of Yucatán's reigning colonial meccas. The paint color known region wide as "Izamal yellow" is a testimony to the ubiquitous and historical yellow-ocher hues that have brushed the city's major facades since colonial times. Also adorning much of the city's exterior architecture are motifs and textures that herald the colonial history of this city: Rajueleado, the use of small chinked stones to pattern and punctuate a stuccoed wall; carved-stone window frames; intricate raised stucco embellishments that incorporate depictions of the Mayan snake and Franciscan's rope. A pilgrimage destination for centuries, Izamal is also home to a sixteenth-century Franciscan convent and the Maya Kinich-Kakmo pyramid.

Situated close to the town's central plaza and convent, Casa de los Artistas is a synchronicity of Izamal's colonial architectural heritage and the early modern Yucatecan houses of the first half of the twentieth century. Artist-owner Claudia Madrazo, architect Salvador Reyes Ríos and designer Josefina Larraín designed Casa de los Artistas to capture the unique color and textural history of Izamal's historic facades.

Originally constructed in the colonial epoch, the home underwent neoclassical updates during the Porfiriato and subsequent updates at the turn of the twentieth century. Previous to Reyes Ríos's original revival, the most recent renovation occurred sometime between 1920 and 1950. The expansion of Casa de los Artistas created four new ample guest rooms/baths, serene outdoor spaces and a rooftop observatory that gives stunning views of the convent and the city's historical facades.

The original L-shaped house opens to the covered corridor and courtyard, and houses two bedrooms/baths and a studio along its length, and the kitchen and open-air dining room are located at the rear end of the property. The addition of two guest rooms behind the house proper defined a patio space between old and new, and showed itself as an ideal area for a tranquil pool and garden area. A second-story addition above the original bedrooms added two more beds/baths, bringing the total to six. A terrace and rooftop observatory above the two new bedrooms culminate the restoration plans.

In its mesmerizing blend of color and texture, the light-filled courtyard of Casa de los Artistas is the central attraction of the property. To celebrate Izamal's distinctive yellow, the walls of the courtyard and its corridors are bathed in the hue that is an ever present reminder of their unique locale. As a tribute to the captivating Mayan stone pyramids outside its doors, carved stone pavers were introduced to the courtyard as flooring.

Standing opposite the covered portal, the boundary wall adjoining the neighboring property was significantly heightened to create more intimacy as well as a canvas for Reyes Ríos's unique "sun clock." In order to minimize the massiveness of the wall, as well as exploit its southern exposure, Reyes Ríos employed three-foot-long hacienda iron rail tracks once used to transport flatbed trucks of henequén fiber from field to machine house. Visibly impaled into the wall's bold yellow stucco, the rails project outward at varying angles. The brilliant effect is of pointed arrows of shadow moving across the wall in response to the changing height and intensity of the sun.

ABOVE: *Nestled between two bedrooms, a tranquil lily pond extends beneath a richly textured, stone-chinked wall. Casa de los Artistas, Yucatán.*

OPPOSITE: *Designed by Salvador Reyes Ríos, a rooftop pergola offers views to Izamal's sixteenth-century convent.*

Concrete floor tiles salvaged
during restoration now serve
as geometric patterned accents
on the central island and
along the counter. A brightly
painted nicho anchors the
space with Oaxacan baskets.
Restoration and design by
Salvador Reyes Ríos and
Josefina Larraín.

The courtyard space was originally conceived as a dry patio that would act as a transition from the front of the house—which opens to a city street—to the newly formed garden, pool and additional two bedrooms in the back of the house. As the project developed, the issue of accommodating the central water cistern beneath the patio needed to be addressed. As an above ground reflection of the water contained below, the new raised water garden provided an aesthetic and functional solution to this challenge. To provide maintenance access to the cistern, iron-frame bases were constructed to sit within a small pond. These bases serve as concealed covers for the cistern, as well as a foundation for sculptural art. The water garden was further integrated to the wall with the addition of an old stone *canal* (rain spout).

PAGES 178–179: *A tranquil pool and textural stone-chinked wall lend contemporary contrast to the back courtyard at Casa de los Artistas, Izamal, Yucatán. Restoration and design by architect Salvador Reyes Ríos.*

ABOVE: *A streamlined concrete counter design incorporates an angled sink and wooden storage shelf, Casa de los Artistas.*

OPPOSITE: *With lush views to the pool, a second floor bedroom features colorful floor tile and a unique suspended bed designed by architect Salvador Reyes Ríos.*

The unique design of the courtyard arches, hewn during the previous restoration, is patterned from the shape made by the corner corbels. Commonly seen in Yucatecan homes from 1920–1950, the arch design inspired Reyes Ríos to echo and re-create the shape throughout the new renovation. As well as using the shape to design the corbels for the newly created kitchen nicho, Reyes Ríos artfully continued the motif in the creation of light sconce fixtures affixed and painted to blend into the front courtyard's columns. Stretching upwards, the sconce in combination with the adjacent two corbels becomes a three-dimensional structure that provides elegant and nondirect lighting for the main walkway. In painted form, the arch design appears on the door frames of the new guest rooms, and its negative image at the top of the free-standing privacy walls dividing showers and toilets in all the home's bathrooms.

Open to the courtyard, the dining room is awash in rich orange hues and features a simple tiled nicho at one end. Once a doorway to the neighboring home, the nicho serves as a patterned repository of a small group of geometric floor tiles salvaged from the home's last renovation. Inside guest bathrooms, small nichos comprised of other remaining floor tile patterns are a featured highlight.

The adjacent original kitchen was redesigned to take advantage of the cross ventilation between the back and front patios. The central polished concrete island, accented with colorful old floor tiles, integrates a new stove as well as storage shelves and drawers. Above the long countertop, a newly created nicho adds drama and warmth with its contrasting golden yellow color and display of Oaxacan baskets.

ABOVE: A *two-toned petate (handwoven palm mat) graces the studio wall at Casa de los Artistas.*

OPPOSITE: *At Casa de los Artistas, artful accents preserve the past: this newly painted wall frames a section of the original wall stencils.*

Testaments to the home's earlier period are also extended in the use of old colonial wall stencils, portions of which were uncovered during the restoration process and highlighted with painted outlines.

Throughout the light-filled rooms, interior decorative elements and furnishings focus on handcrafted artistry. In collaboration with John Powell and Josh Ramos, Reyes Ríos and Larraín blended comfortable wood and leather chairs with more contemporary pieces, including side tables crafted from black strap-iron. Balancing the sea of yellow flooring and walls, black was used in combination with the golden floor tiles to create a strong geometric path guiding visitors to the back of the property. The newly crafted iron window grilles lining the corridor enhance this counterbalance, as do the sculptural strap-iron lamps, tables and wrought-iron beds. A two-toned petate graces the studio wall and pillows crafted from intricately embroidered *huipiles* (women's blouses) punctuate a bold red sofa.

ABOVE: A *nicho framed in carved stone features an artful sculpture*, Casa Marisol, Mérida, Yucatán.

OPPOSITE: *Original ornate stucco ornamentation decorates the elegant arches at Casa Marisol*, Mérida, Yucatán.

Casa Marisol

At Casa Marisol, a restored colonial-style home in downtown Mérida, elegant arches and stone columns surround a palm-filled courtyard, cascading water fountain and inviting pool. Dating from 1888, the house is listed on Mexico's historical register and features 21-foot-high ceilings and unique architectural details. Over the years, the building housed local businesses and was partly unoccupied since 1960, when it last served as a residence.

For the home's extensive restoration, owners Ron and Sylvia Jackson collaborated with architect Alvaro Ponce and skilled local craftsmen to revitalize the home's original features which included old doors, colorful concrete floor tiles and ornate stucco ornamentation on the inner arches.

The height of the kitchen's sculptural stove hood was raised for increased function with the Talavera-tiled countertop. Today, the rich red of the hood and its dramatic height anchor the red-themed kitchen dressed in red, white, gold and blue tiles selected by Sylvia Jackson.

Known for residential designs that seamlessly integrate nature into living spaces, Ponce worked closely with the Jacksons to create a strong indoor-outdoor relationship throughout the house. The home's light-filled bathroom owes its brightness to floor-to-ceiling glass walls that allow one to inhabit the courtyard space from inside. In addition to opening onto the central courtyard's inviting waterfall and pool, the master bathroom suite opens to a lush private garden featuring trickling water fountains, an outdoor shower and a hammock-strung pergola. Surrounded by tropical gardens, the backyard *palapa*—replete with outdoor kitchen—is a favored entertaining area at Casa Marisol where the Jacksons enjoy spending time with family and friends.

Inside and out, Casa Marisol features natural textures of local stone. Ponce used the Yucatán tradition of rajueleado to add decorative interest to key wall surfaces. The technique utilizes small, hand-cut stones chinked from larger stones, creating a mesmerizing textural statement. A natural, orange-hued Ticul stone was used for the chinked walls, as well as for the courtyard's rough-cut, square stone tiles. The color of the warm orange walls was attained by Ponce's special recipe that mixes natural pigments with water, applied in multiple coats with a henequén brush.

Lending contrast to interior and courtyard walls, a cream-white stone called *Crema Maya* was used for door and nicho surrounds and flooring. *Conchuela*, or fossil stone, was employed for water fountain spouts. Ceiling beams of *pucte* (tropical hardwood) balance the stone textures beneath the portal and inside rooms.

Inside, arched nichos spotlight the Jacksons' extensive collection of art objects and Mexican Talavera pieces, hand-painted pots from Chiapas and fine Mayan reproductions of pre-Hispanic ceramics. Antiques and comfortable Mexican furniture blend well with Moroccan kilims and embroidered pillows from Chiapas.

The fulfilling collaboration between the Jacksons and Alvaro Ponce on Casa Marisol engendered a business partnership—*Yucatán Sol*—born of their mutual interest in utilizing the richness of local materials and artisans in the renovations of colonial homes. The company specializes in architectural elements and construction methods that have evolved from regional hacienda influences and age-old Mayan traditions.

OPPOSITE: A *dramatic sculptural stove hood anchors the red-hued, Talavera-tiled kitchen at Casa Marisol in Mérida. A vaulted brick ceiling lends additional interest to the grand-scale colorful room.*

ABOVE: A *kitchen nicho is decorated in Talavera tile, Casa Marisol, Yucatán.*

Hacienda Granada

DESIGNING OUR OWN HACIENDA HOME WAS THE NATURAL CONCLUSION OF OUR MANY YEARS' WORK VISITING, RESEARCHING AND PHOTOGRAPHING MEXICO'S UNIQUE HACIENDA ESTATES. Immersing ourselves in the restoration of an eighteenth-century Mexican hacienda, we became intimate with the unique architectural elements, colors and handcrafted textures showcased in our previous books. With the knowledge and inspiration gained through these endeavors, we knew we were prepared to bring the rich hacienda design aesthetic home to our own residential project in Texas.

Numerous design details peculiar to old Mexican architecture have intrigued us for decades: centuries-old, nail-studded doors creaking open to a covered záguan and interior courtyard; turned-spindle window guards against earthen red walls; arcaded portales punctuated with wall-embedded, wooden hammock hooks; carved stone canales (rainspouts) casting striking shadows across rich yellow ocher walls; hand-wrought iron *faroles* (lanterns); cool, colored floor tiles; and sinks hewn from stone. These and other images born of old world Mexico spawned the design plans that eventually became Hacienda Granada, our Texas home.

◆◆◆◆◆◆◆◆◆◆

OPPOSITE: *Old Mexican hacienda doors open onto an arcaded courtyard and záguan. Hacienda Granada, Texas.*

ABOVE: *Mexican lanterns are supported by decorative wrought-iron brackets.*

We found secluded acreage resplendent with tall, mature oak trees, a substantial limestone outcropping and a creek that promised well for our project. The slight slope of the land, however, presented a number of challenges in siting the house. To allow the building's scale and roofline to blend well with the sloping, heavily-treed terrain of the hill country,

certain modifications were made with ceiling heights. The advantages of abundant space and lack of zoning restrictions luckily outweighed the problems we faced in accommodating our desired one-story, 100-foot by 67-foot design with the sloped terrain and required creek setbacks. However, the excavation costs were not minimal.

PREVIOUS SPREAD: Hacienda Granada is rich with myriad natural textures including handmade Mexican clay bricks, stone rainspouts and clay roof tiles. An old Oaxaca ceramic and stone water filter (upside down) tops an antique Mexican table.

THIS PAGE: A Oaxacan bench and antique ceramic grace the colorful záguan at Hacienda Granada.

OPPOSITE: Once paired with an antique santo a brass corona rests above a colonial trunk and custom wrought-iron stand.

Having visited many haciendas that were designed around a central courtyard, we knew we wanted the feel of a defined, open-air space that was visible from all the house's rooms. Equally important was creating the feel of an old home, which we attained through the use of old architectural elements as well as handcrafted materials, finishes and traditional colors.

THIS PAGE: Once used on a
Mexican hacienda for feeding
livestock, this old trough is one
solid piece of sabino wood.

OPPOSITE: Found on an
old ranch in Mexico, a carved
mortero (mortar) is now
used as a sculptural planter.

We chose to design Hacienda Granada around an enclosed courtyard accessed by a traditional záguan. A few steps inside the nine-foot-tall eighteenth-century *portones* reveal a golden-yellow courtyard whose perimeter is marked by a 65-foot-long arcaded portal wrapping around three sides. The fourth, south side is bound by a tall 16-foot wall that is alive with shadow play from palms and bamboo. Handmade in northern Mexico, golden yellow and red clay bricks complemented our *barro rojo*, or red clay, exterior limepaint color and the yellow ocher courtyard hue, their earthy red and golden cream tones offering an interesting textural surface for both courtyard and portal.

Once the design was defined, we collaborated with architect Gina Andre of Acanthus Architecture to fine-tune our design into working drawings. Priorities included finding a suitable angle for the shed roof and incorporating the use of wooden ceiling beams throughout the hacienda. Builder Micky Maness of Coachman Homes easily integrated our custom requests, which included deep alacenas (built-in wall cabinets), a large arched nicho and decorative details, such as antique stone elements that were set into the walls around the courtyard.

We chose to build with an insulated concrete form system as it produces a monolithic reinforced concrete wall that is structurally sound, energy efficient and fire retardant. Not least, the wall mass created by using ICF instills a feeling of solidity found only in well-made adobe structures or old rubblestone haciendas. The nine arches for our arcaded portal were hand "sculpted" from ICF blocks which, once in place, were filled with concrete to complete the sturdy building system.

PAGE 198: *Hacienda
Granada's dining room is
resplendent with rich color,
wrought-iron sconces, Mexican
concrete tile and an alacena
with antique doors. Custom
antique pine dining table.
Design by Joe P. Carr and
Karen Witynski.*

PAGE 199: *Hacienda
Granada's alacena opens to
reveal a collection of antique
Mexican and Guatemalan
ceramics. Lockplate sconces
highlight rich, colorful walls.
Pittsburgh® Paints, The Voice
of Color® Delta Clay, 127-7.*

ABOVE: A *colonial* retablo
*in its original green tin frame
hangs in the colorful kitchen at
Hacienda Granada.*

OPPOSITE: *The dining
room's antique Mexican doors
feature turned spindles which
provide a view to the bright
cocina at Hacienda Granada.*

Mexico's traditional alacenas, or built-in wall cabinets, present a
streamlined storage solution while providing a unique showcase for old
doors. Commonly raised off the floor 12 to 16 inches, alacenas are also a
good use of shorter antique doors that may not meet building codes for
standard doorway use.

Especially inspired by the alacenas we encountered at Hacienda
Temozón in the Yucatán, we designed alacenas into the dining room and
office. In the *comedor* (dining room), a pair of colonial doors—originally
painted white but stripped to reveal natural wood tones—now front a
seven-foot-tall alacena that serves as a cocktail bar with a lighted display
of antique Mexican and Guatemalan pottery. On the end wall of our
office, a 24-inch-deep alacena is raised 15 inches off the floor, and plays
host to books and Oaxacan palm baskets that conceal fabric and leather
samples for clients.

Inspired by the beautifully tiled, seventeenth-century Puebla convent kitchens and the grand-scale design of the semicircular kitchen island at Hacienda San Gabriel de las Palmas in Morelos, we designed a shapely, massive island into our cocina plans. It provides a dramatic focal point for the room and allows for a grand-scale surface in which to mix tile patterns. Working with a full-scale template of the counterfront, we designed the overall pattern by mixing our favorite Talavera-style tiles in blue, white and yellow.

In old hacienda days, the centuries-old curved island shape accommodated a number of burners along the countertop, easing the task of preparing meals for hundreds of people. Though multiple burners no longer extend the length of today's island countertops, the extra space this original shape provides allows for placement of a range and oven. We chose a dual-fuel range with downdraft feature, providing a gas cooktop and electric oven.

To balance the strong dose of golden yellow from the kitchen floor tiles, we chose a soothing, cream-white tone for the walls, finished with a centuries-old plaster mixture that provides a beautiful luster that reflects natural light. With expert skill, a talented team of Oaxacan artisans added juice of the nopal cactus into the final coat of the lime plaster, then hand-burnished the walls to provide the lustrous finish. This plaster recipe and application technique is the same as used during the restoration of the renowned sixteenth-century Santo Domingo Convent in Oaxaca.

Hacienda Granada's colorful cocina features a poured concrete countertop and island decorated with traditional, Mexican glazed tiles. Antique Talavera tiles add interest to the nicho behind the sink. Design by Karen Witynski and Joe P. Carr.

Hacienda Granada's sala features Mexican colonial antiques, old ceramics and comfortable furnishings. A Rodolfo Morales pastel hangs above the simple fireplace. Design by Joe P. Carr and Karen Witynski.

An eighteenth-century arcón
*(trunk) from Ecuador anchors
Hacienda Granada's sala.
Mr. Puppy keeps a watchful
eye on Mexican dance masks
and antique painted crosses.*

ABOVE: A *rarely seen detail accents a very old ceramic pot from Oaxaca.*

OPPOSITE: *Three Mexican colonial trunks and old doors add old-world elegance to Hacienda Granada's sala.*

PAGES 210–211: *A poured concrete countertop supports red travertine sinks inspired by Mexican stone troughs. Onyx sconces illuminate the arched, free-standing wall. Pittsburgh® Paints, The Voice of Color® Pralines and Cream, 117-3. Design by Joe P. Carr and Karen Witynski, Hacienda Granada, Texas.*

The colored coolness of concrete tile floors in spacious haciendas and colonial homes we visited inspired our choice to use concrete tiles from two of our favorite Yucatán tile sources, Mosaicos Traqui and Mosaicos La Peninsular. Their rich color palette and reservoir of colonial patterns is a refreshing alternative to the more commonly used fired clay tiles or travertine. Golden yellow, 12-inch tiles imbue our kitchen with a warm glow, complementing the glazed tiles on the counter and island.

In the dining room, a geometric mix of solid agate-blue and cream tiles underfoot softens the bold effect of the papaya-hued walls. For the photo archive room, we custom-colored an old colonial tile pattern to coordinate with the rooms' painted antique doors. The overall pattern is created by joining four, 8-inch square green, white and deep red tiles, laid within a field of solid antique white tiles for contrast. For our sala, we chose a *moreno* (dark) saltillo tile, as its chocolate color compliments our espresso-hued sofas and offers an alternative to the more traditional red and golden saltillo tile seen throughout the southwest. The dark tile also offers a counterbalance to the soft, golden-hued walls achieved with a custom limewash from Portola Paints.

Our collection of colonial antique furniture also factored into the design choices for the sala, as we desired a color palette to compliment two cherished pieces: a seventeenth-century Ecuadorian, seven-foot long arcón, or trunk, and a 200-year-old mesquite carpenter's table whose thick planks have developed a deep dark patina, the latter becoming an anchor piece behind one of the sofas. Additionally, a Mexican triangular candelabra and collection of tall, sculptural sugar molds also blend well with the moreno tile.

Our preference for minimally furnished interiors led us to devise a way in which our collection of Mexican masks could be displayed without resorting to the typical wall or tabletop presentation. We designed the sala's end wall to be built out at the bottom to create a 54-inch-high by 10-inch-deep ledge the entire length of the wall, creating a subtle shelf to allow for interchanging art displays without the use of furniture.

In addition to the pair of portones on the front entrance, we found antique doors to reiterate the feeling of aged, hand-wrought texture throughout the home. In keeping with the grand-style proportions of long hacienda salas (living rooms) that extend to join separate dining rooms, our dining room and sala are a continuous space. An antique pair of raised panel doors, however, creates a frame for each room and an arched pair of nine-foot-tall, arched spindled doors provides an open view between dining room and kitchen.

The additional interior doors for bedrooms, bathrooms, pantry and laundry are from our hacienda door collection, crafted in Mexico using old-world, hand-adzed methods and featuring hand-wrought iron clavos (large, round nail heads). Stained a dark coffee tone, the doors are crafted from kiln-dried white cedar and feature old-style mustache hinges. For the rooms that open onto the courtyard, we used windowed heart-pine doors to increase light.

In the main bathroom, rectangular stone troughs once used for watering livestock inspired the design of the pair of bathroom sinks. Carved from Mexican red travertine, the sinks blend brown with deep red tones. Twelve-inch stone tiles in red and orange-brown tones cover both floor and walls. Baños in the restored Yucatán haciendas we visited were minimally partitioned; a design layout that we desired to replicate. To convert the tall-ceilinged rooms into functional bathrooms allowing privacy between the shower and WC, we based an arched, free-standing wall into the room's center. Fronting this wall is the sink counter, and a perpendicular divider behind it separates shower and WC. A poured concrete bathtub complements the room's height and sink counter.

Hacienda Granada's office wall features an alacena with raised-panel doors. An old Mexican copete (crest) and Guatemalan children's chairs accent the alacena. Pittsburgh® Paints, The Voice of Color® Golden Mushroom, 216-2. Design by Joe P. Carr and Karen Witynski.

Old stone rings, used for tying up horses, were embedded in walls adjacent to watering troughs or near hacienda entrances. Years ago, we found two of these rings extracted from a restoration project. We knew someday they would again be put to use, integrated into a wall for textural interest. Today, one holds court in our central courtyard and the other postures in close proximity to our eighteenth-century front doors.

Resources

We invite you to visit our gallery, **Joe P. Carr Design**, for Mexican colonial antiques and hacienda style elements, including old doors, wrought-iron window grilles, ceiling beams and flooring. In addition to colonial trunks, benches, tables, chairs and armoires, we also offer an exclusive line of iron lockplate sconces, lanterns and chandeliers. Our hacienda doors are hand-crafted in Mexico and are available in custom sizes. Decorative accents include antique ceramics, rare Mexican textiles, culinary antiques and old stone elements. Design services available.

Please visit our website for Mexican design news:

www.mexicanstyle.com

Authors' Mailing Address:
JOE P. CARR &
KAREN WITYNSKI
3267 Bee Caves Rd. #107-181
Austin, TX 78746
512 370-9663
512 327-8284
www.mexicanstyle.com

Authors' Gallery:
JOE P. CARR DESIGN
3601 Bee Caves Road
at Barton Springs Nursery
Austin, TX 78746
512 370-9663
512 327-8284

KAREN WITYNSKI
Architectural &
Interior Photography
512 370-9663
512 327-8284

TOP: *Authors Joe P. Carr and Karen Witynski.*

ABOVE: *Traditional Yucatán door with grilled shutters.*

OPPOSITE: *Old colonial doors, furniture and decorative accents available at Joe P. Carr Design.*

ARCHITECTS & BUILDERS

REYES RIOS+LARRAIN
Restoration, Architecture,
Design & Landscape
Salvador Reyes Ríos
Josefina Larraín
Mérida, Yucatán
999 923-5808
reyesrios@prodigy.net.mx

PLAN ARQUITECTOS
Luis Bosoms C., Architect
Mexico City, Mexico
555 257-0097
luis.bosoms@grupoplan.com
www.grupoplan.com

CARDENAS ARQUITECTOS
Mérida, Yucatán
999 920-3578
cardenasarquitectos@hotmail.com

MICKY MANESS, Builder
COACHMAN HOMES INC.
512 844-5843
www.coachmanhomesinc.com

ALVARO PONCE, Architect
Mérida, Yucatán
999 943-3075
corvina@tponce.com

HENRY PONCE, Architect
Mérida, Yucatán
999 926-0018
ponce_henry@yahoo.com

MANOLO VEGA
Builder/Designer
Mérida, Yucatán
999 970-1298
mvega62@prodigy.net.mx

HERNAN PIMENTEL, Architect
Pátzcuaro, Michoacán
434 342-1098

DANIEL LOPEZ SALGADO, Architect
Oaxaca, Oaxaca
951 132-4290

LOGAN WAGNER, Architect
Austin, Texas
512 441-9729

DESIGNERS

SALVADOR REYES RIOS
JOSEFINA LARRAIN
Furniture Design, Tile/Color Design
Mérida, Yucatán
999 923-5808
jlarrain@sureste.com

WISECRACKER DESIGN
Jim Neeley + David Dow
jimneeley@aol.com
www.casapocitoyucatan.com

URBANO DESIGN SERVICES
Josh Ramos and John Powell
Mérida, Yucatán
999 924-4145
www.bestofyucatan.com

RAYMOND BRANHAM
Artist/Designer
Mérida, Yucatán
999 924-0208
raymondbranham@hotmail.com

CARLOS MILLET CAMARA
Designer/Artist
Mérida,Yucatán
999 944-1082

JOE P. CARR DESIGN
Joe P. Carr / Karen Witynski
Austin, Texas &
Mérida, Yucatán
512 327-8284
512 370-9663
www.mexicanstyle.com

Paint Color

HACIENDA STYLE COLOR PALETTE
PITTSBURGH® PAINTS

The Hacienda Style Color Palette reflects
the rustic elegance of Mexico's old-world, country estates
and their rich cultural history. Color cards available.

www.pittsburghpaints.com
www.thevoiceofcolor.com

Technical & Customer Support:
1 800 441-9695

RESOURCES

Floor Tile

MOSAICOS TRAQUI
Mérida, Yucatán
988 916-1500
traquin84@prodigy.net.mx

MOSAICOS LA PENINSULAR
Mérida, Yucatán
999 923-1196
www.paginasprodigy.com/mosaico
speninsular

FOLK ART

HECHO A MANO
Izamal, Yucatán
988 954-0344

AMATE BOOKS & FOLK ART
951 516-3935 - Oaxaca
999 924-2222 - Yucatán
www.amatebooks.com

ARTISTS

FERNANDO CASTRO PACHECO
Mérida, Yucatán
999 924-4799

JAIME BARRERA AGUILAR
jabaguilar@prodigy.net.mx

THIS PAGE: *Old Mexican*
crosses and a colonial armoire.
Collection of the authors.

BOOKS

Haciendas de Mexico
Ricardo Rendón Garcini
Fomento Cultural Banamex, A.C., 1994

Vida Cotidiana en Las Haciendas de Mexico
Ricardo Rendón Garcini
Fomento Cultural Banamex, A.C., 1997

Traditional Mexican Cooking
Adela Fernández
Panorama Editorial
www.panoramaed.com.mx

Arquitectura de Las Haciendas Henequeneras
Roberto Ancona Riestra
Universidad Autónoma de Yucatán,
1996

Early Mexican Houses
Richard G. Garrison and
George Rustay
Architectural Book Publishing Co.
1930

La Casa Que Canta
Mariana Yampolsky
Mexico City, SEP, 1982

TRADEMARKS

Pittsburgh® Paints and The
Voice of Color® are registered
trademarks of PPG Architectural
Finishes, Inc.

REAL ESTATE

TIERRA YUCATAN
Mérida, Yucatán
999 923-7615
999 930-9684
www.tierra-maya.com

The Yucatán's colonial charms include the city of Izamal (below), Hacienda Santa Rosa (right) and Hacienda San Antonio Cucul (bottom).

Travel Guide

MEXICO'S CAPTIVATING COLONIAL CITIES are an attractive destination offering visitors architectural splendor amidst elegant 18th-century hotels and restored hacienda resorts. Continental Airlines flies to 30 Mexico destinations–including key colonial cities–more than any other U.S. carrier. Continental also offers more flights from the U.S. to Mexico than any other carrier.

U.S. Reservations (800) 231-0856
Mexico Reservations 01 (800) 900-5000
www.continental.com

Continental Airlines

HACIENDAS

THE HACIENDAS
THE LUXURY COLLECTION
OWNERS: GRUPO PLAN

Hacienda San José Cholul, Yucatán
Hacienda Santa Rosa, Yucatán
Hacienda Temozón, Yucatán
Hacienda Ochil, Yucatán
Hacienda Uayamón, Campeche
Hacienda Puerta Campeche
Managed by:
Starwood Hotels & Resorts
999 923-8089
1 800 325-3589 toll free in U.S.
www.luxurycollection.com

HACIENDA XCANATUN
Mérida, Yucatán
999 941-0213
www.xcanatun.com

HACIENDA TEYA
Hotel—Restaurant—Events
Mérida, Yucatán
999 988-0800
www.haciendateya.com

HACIENDA SAN ANTONIO
Tixkokob, Yucatán
999 910-6144
www.haciendasanantonio.com.mx

HACIENDA SANTA CRUZ
Yucatán
999 910-4549
www.haciendasantacruz.com

HACIENDA SOTUTA DE PEÓN
Special Tour—
Yucatán Henequen Hacienda
999 941-8639
www.haciendatour.com

HACIENDA DE CORTES
Cuernavaca, Morelos
777 315-8844
www.hotelhaciendadecortes.com

HACIENDA DE SAN ANTONIO
Colima, Colima
312 313-4229
www.haciendadesanantonio.com

HACIENDA DE LOS SANTOS
Alamos, Sonora
647 428-0222
www.haciendadelossantos.com

HACIENDA LOS LAURELES
Oaxaca, Oaxaca
951 501-5300
www.hotelhaciendaloslaureles.com

ABOVE: *The inviting arcade at
La Mision de Fray Diego hotel in
Mérida, Yucatán.*

COLONIAL STYLE HOTELS

LA MISION DE FRAY DIEGO
Mérida, Yucatán
999 924-1111
www.lamisiondefraydiego.com

HOTEL MARIONETAS
Mérida, Yucatán
999 928-3377
www.hotelmarionetas.com

**LOS DOS COOKING SCHOOL
& GUESTHOUSE**
Mérida, Yucatán
999 928-1116
www.los-dos.com

CASA SANTANA
Mérida, Yucatán
999 928-7567
www.casasantana.com

**ANGELES DE MERIDA
BED & BREAKFAST**
Mérida, Yucatán
999 923-8163
www.angelesdemerida.com

**VILLA MARIA
RESTAURANT & HOTEL**
Mérida, Yucatán
999 923-3357
www.villamariamerida.com

HOTEL MEDIO MUNDO
Mérida, Yucatán
999 924-5472
www.hotelmediomundo.com

CASA COLONIAL
Mérida, Yucatán
999 924-5927
www.yucatanproductions.com

HOTEL LA CASONA DE TITA
Oaxaca, Oaxaca
951 516-1402
www.hotellacasonadetitaoaxaca.com.mx

OTHER FAVORITES

CASA NALUM
Riviera Maya, Quintana Roo
984 806-4905
www.nalum.com

**FUNDACION HACIENDAS
EN EL MUNDO MAYA**
Mérida, Yucatán: 999 928-7750
Mexico City: 555 257-0097
www.haciendasmundomaya.com

OTHER KEY HACIENDAS
HACIENDA ITZINCAB CAMARA
HACIENDA SAN ANTONIO CUCUL
HACIENDA CHICHI DE LOS LAGOS
HACIENDA DE SAN LORENZO DE AKE
HACIENDA CHENKU
HACIENDA KANKABCHEN
HACIENDA POXILA
HACIENDA CHICHI SUAREZ
HACIENDA CHIMAY

YUCATAN TOURISM OFFICE
www.mayayucatan.com

ABOVE: *The elegant dining
room at Villa Maria Restaurant
features colonial tile and richly
painted walls, Mérida, Yucatán.*

OPPOSITE: *Authors Karen
and Joe on location in Mexico
with friends Rene and Juan.*

MEXICAN DESIGN BOOK SERIES
by KAREN WITYNSKI & JOE P. CARR

Hacienda Dogs

CLOCKWISE FROM TOP LEFT: *Hacienda Itzincab's beloved dogs; Mr. Puppy at Hacienda Granada, the authors' residence; Balzac taking a siesta at Hacienda Yodzonot, Yucatán.*